A TREASURY OF
TITANIC TALES

A TREASURY OF
TITANIC TALES

WEBB GARRISON

Rutledge Hill Press®
Nashville, Tennessee

Published in Nashville, Tennessee, by Rutledge Hill Press®, 211 Seventh Avenue North, Nashville, Tennessee 37219. Distributed in Canada by H. B. Fenn & Company, Ltd., 34 Nixon Road, Bolton, Ontario L7E 1W2.

Typography by E. T. Lowe, Nashville, Tennessee.

Library of Congress Cataloging-in-Publication Data

Garrison, Webb B.
    A treasury of Titanic tales / Webb Garrison.
      p. cm.
    Includes bibliographical references and index.
    ISBN 1-55853-658-2 (pbk.)
    1. Titanic (Steamship)—History.   2. Shipwrecks—North Atlantic Ocean—History. I. Title.
    G530.T6G375   1998
    910'.91634—dc21   98-20438
                                             CIP

Printed in the United States of America.

2 3 4 5 6 7 8 9—00 99 98

Contents

Introduction

ALTHOUGH DISASTERS of many kinds have occurred since the beginning of recorded history, none has captured the world's imagination like the sinking of the *Titanic*. Two major factors contribute to this uniqueness.

First, the vessel was heralded in the press as "unsinkable," although her designers never made that claim. She was considered to be invulnerable to forces that could overcome ordinary ships, the crowning peak of human achievement. More than simply a floating palace or a grand hotel on the sea, the length of the *Titanic* exceeded the height of the tallest buildings, making it the largest movable object constructed up to that time. That so magnificent an achievement could be lost as a result of contact with ordinary ice was monstrous and unthinkable. Perhaps that is why so many people found it incomprehensible that she had gone to the bottom on her maiden voyage.

Second, the first-class passengers aboard the liner on this cruise represented a concentration of wealth and influence like none other previously assembled. When the icy waters of the North Atlantic claimed the lives of numerous multimillionaires, several of the world's greatest private fortunes changed hands in a matter of hours.

There is a widespread but mistaken belief that the number of casualties from the loss of the *Titanic* was record-setting. At the close of the U.S. Civil War, a scruffy old steamer named the *Sultana* was chugging up the Mississippi River grossly overloaded with Union veterans and prisoners of war finally released by the surrender of the South. The vessel blew up not far from Memphis and almost certainly accounted for more deaths than the tragedy of the *Titanic*. Estimates of the death toll when the ocean liner sank vary only slightly, but in the case of the riverboat, a review by a special body created by the U.S. Army announced that 1,238 persons died on April 27, 1865. Not so, according to the U.S. Customs Service at Memphis; officials there claimed that at least 1,547 lives were lost on that otherwise tranquil night.

The loss of the *Titanic* made major headlines throughout the Western world for weeks, while the loss of the *Sultana* was barely noted. The luxurious ocean liner was transporting persons whom many labeled "important"; the decrepit river steamer was crowded with former soldiers who were described as "obscure ordinary men." The *Sultana* disaster was also somewhat overshadowed by the news of the apprehension and death of the assassin of Abraham Lincoln, John Wilkes Booth.

To take a fresh look at the 1912 disaster in the North Atlantic, therefore, it is essential to do more than enumerate the rich and famous who perished or were saved. In these pages, an attempt is made to evoke three-dimensional portraits of some of those involved with the story. One notable who did not die during that night of cold terror has been neglected in earlier chronicles of the ill-fated ship. Had it not been for Italian scientist-inventor Guglielmo Marconi and his new "wireless telegraphy," it's unlikely that a single passenger or crew member would have been saved.

Three survivors wrote valuable accounts of their experiences. Second-class passenger Lawrence Beesley's is the most precise, Second Officer Charles Lightoller's is the most sea-oriented, and Col. Archibald Gracie's includes the most information about the men and women in first class. All of these accounts are "must reading" for anyone hoping to begin to understand the ship, her passengers, and her five-day voyage into infamy.

An immense amount of on-the-spot material is available in other sources. The *New York Times* and the *London Daily Sketch* contributed more to this collection of vignettes than all of the splendid books that have been written about the *Titanic*.

Will some future catastrophe become more memorable than the loss of the great ocean liner? Probably not. The mystique of the ship and those aboard her promises to become more fascinating, not less, as time goes by.

A TREASURY OF
TITANIC TALES

1

HAROLD BRIDE

SWITCHED SIGNALS

AT AGE twenty-one, Harold Bride's experience was limited. He watched and listened intently, however, as twenty-five-year-old Jack Phillips tapped out a distress signal. When there was no reply, Bride deferentially suggested, "Why not try the *American* call?"

Just after midnight on April 12, 1912, the modified signal went out. Neither Bride nor Phillips had the slightest idea that the seemingly trifling change would save the junior Marconi wireless operator's life and more than seven hundred others.

Aboard the steamer *Carpathia* ten minutes after she docked in New York, Bride was speechless when he was introduced to his employer, the great Guglielmo Marconi, by a *New York Times* reporter. A few hours later he stared incredulously at page one of the paper's April 16 issue. Spread across four columns, an account of the sinking of the most splendid vessel in the world did not identify the professional newsman who prepared it. Instead, it informed readers that the story was "by Harold Bride, surviving wireless operator of the *Titanic.*"

Although he had no personal knowledge of the workings of a metropolitan daily, Bride was sure he had never before seen a story credited to a person not on the staff of the newspaper. His account constituted "the biggest personal experience story of the twentieth century" he later learned.

The article began with Bride's stressing his awareness that wireless operators aboard the rescue ship had sent no details about the disaster to stations on shore because hundreds of "personal messages with words of grief" demanded all of the operators' time. Some details about the awesome night of April 14 did go to the ship *Chester.* When relayed to shore, said Bride, these messages were almost useless because the operators on the *Chester* were unskilled and did not know the Continental Morse code, which was significantly different from the less widely used American Morse.

When rescued by being dragged to the deck of the *Carpathia,* Bride was sent to the sick bay for medical treatment. After nearly half a day there, he was informed that the only wireless operator aboard the rescue vessel had worked so long and intensely that he was "getting queer" and had to have relief. Using crutches, the young survivor climbed the ladder to the transmitting station, took over the brass key of the sending instrument, "and never left the wireless cabin after that" until reaching New York.

He castigated operators aboard U.S. Navy vessels that were within range of his apparatus as "a great nuisance." All of them, said the native of England who had less than a year of experience with the Marconi Company, should learn Continental Morse and gain a great deal more speed. "We worked all the time," he insisted. "Nothing went wrong. Sometimes the *Carpathia* man sent, and sometimes I sent. There was a bed in the wireless cabin. I could sit on it and rest my feet while sending sometimes."

A Rude Awakening

Bride first worked for the Marconi Company on the *Hoverford* and then transferred to the *Lusitania,* which was believed to be the fastest passenger steamer afloat. When construction of the White Star Line's *Titanic* was completed at Belfast, he was ordered to go aboard the gigantic new luxury liner. Phillips, the senior wireless operator, instructed Bride to relieve him for a few hours after midnight each night. That meant he had much idle time, and so he slept more than usual.

On Sunday, however, the wireless broke down and Bride went to work early. He and Phillips spent several hours trying to repair the system and eventually found that a small component called a "secretary" had burned out. Their apparatus was functioning again, only a few hours before the ship hit the iceberg.

On the big ship, the wireless cabin had three rooms instead of the single room found on smaller vessels. One room was set aside for the dynamo that powered the wireless, another was equipped with a bunk, and the third was used to operate the communications system.

THRILLING STORY BY TITANIC'S SURVIVING WIRELESS MAN
Bride Tells How He and Phillips Worked and How He Finished a Stoker Who Tried to Steal Phillips's Life Belt—Ship Sank to Tune of "Autumn"
BY HAROLD BRIDE, SURVIVING WIRELESS OPERATOR OF THE TITANIC.

Guglielmo Marconi himself brokered the arrangement with the New York Times *that gave the newspaper exclusive rights to the firsthand accounts of the two wireless operators, Harold S. Bride of the* Titanic *and Harold Cottam of the* Carpathia.

On Sunday evening Bride turned in early so he could sleep a few hours before relieving his superior, who was weary from the tedious repair job but had hundreds of messages from passengers to send to shore. After a brief nap, the young Englishman roused and heard Phillips sending message after message to a receiving station on Cape Race. All of them dealt with "traffic matters," or personal concerns of the affluent passengers in first class. Concerned about his comrade's weariness, Bride crawled out of his bunk without dressing and took over the key.

"I didn't even feel the shock" when the ship hit, he declared. "I hardly knew it had happened until the captain put his head in the cabin and told us we had struck an iceberg. Although damage was probably slight, he had ordered a ship-wide inspection to assess it. 'You better get ready to send out a call for assistance,' he told Bride. 'But don't send it until I tell you.' "

Ten minutes after Capt. Edward J. Smith returned to the bridge of the ship there was terrible confusion outside the wireless cabin. The noise was so great that in spite of being bone-weary, Phillips woke up and wanted to know what had happened. Just then the captain put his head in the door and ordered: "Send the call for assistance."

Startled, Phillips wanted to know what call he should send.

"The regulation international call for help. Just that," responded Smith, a veteran of forty-three years at sea. Called back into service from semiretirement to take the *Titanic* across the Atlantic on her maiden voyage, Smith was one of the most respected and admired captains on the sea.

As Bride later told his employer and the newspaper reporter who had managed to reach him, "Phillips began to send CQD. He flashed

Harold Bride was the junior Marconi operator aboard the Titanic. *He was twenty-one years old and had been with the wireless company for eighteen months at the time of the disaster.*

away at it and we joked while he did so. Both of us made light of the disaster. We joked while he flashed signals for about five minutes."

Captain Smith then returned, visibly perturbed, and demanded to know what signal was being transmitted. When Phillips replied "CQD," Bride broke into the conversation. "Try sending an SOS," he suggested. "It's the new call, and it may be your only chance to send it." Both he and Phillips knew that the standard distress call in the version of the Morse code usually used in England and Europe meant "call to quarters" (invitation to talk) and "distress."

Chuckling, the senior operator changed his call for help to the American version. Captain Smith informed the Marconi men that the ship had apparently struck an iceberg amidships. Both wireless operators, who had noticed only a slight jolt, thought they had passed the obstacle and were now away from it.

"We said lots of funny things to each other in the next few minutes," Bride continued. After picking up the *Frankfurd,* they gave her their position and asked for help as a result of having hit an iceberg. Instead of replying immediately, the operator on the German liner left his post to give the news to his captain. By the time he returned, the *Titanic* was "sinking by the head," causing a distinct forward list of the decks.

No promise of help came from the *Frankfurd,* but when the operator on the *Carpathia* received the distress message, he informed his captain. Five minutes later he reported back that the Cunard Line steamer was "putting about and heading for us."

John "Jack" Phillips was the senior Marconi operator aboard the Titanic. *He had celebrated his twenty-fifth birthday on April 11, the first day of the ship's maiden voyage. Phillips had been with British Marconi for six years, having graduated at the top of his class at the training school in Liverpool. Marconi reputedly hand-picked him for the position aboard the* Titanic.

Commotion among Passengers

Phillips instructed Bride to hurry to the bridge and report the message from the *Carpathia*. "I did so," the junior member of the wireless team recalled, "and I went through an awful mass of people. The decks were full of scrambling men and women. I saw no fighting but I [later] heard tell of it." Until he returned to his post, he did not notice that he had failed to dress. Once clothed, he took an overcoat to the senior operator and placed it over his shoulders while he continued to work the massive brass key. At short intervals, Bride was sent back to Captain Smith with brief messages that included the position and speed of the *Carpathia*.

With the forward list becoming sharper, Bride saw women and children scrambling into the lifeboats. By this time wireless signals from the stricken vessel were becoming weaker as water poured into the engine rooms. Captain Smith returned once more to warn that the dynamos might go out soon, so that message was flashed to the rescue ship that was on its way.

Although the water was rapidly approaching the boat deck, Phillips stayed at his post. "He was a brave man," Bride recalled.

The White Star Line spared no expense in assembling one of the finest ship's orchestras afloat. Wallace Hartley (above center), the bandmaster and violinist, had been lured from Cunard. Jock Hume (bottom, right), second violinist, took the position because it paid well and he was soon to be married. Pianist Theodore Brailey (middle left) and cellist Roger Bricoux (above right) had come on board from the Carpathia. Fred Clark (bottom left), the bass viol player, had never been to sea before. George Krins (viola, above left), J. W. Woodward (cello, middle right), and P. C. Taylor (piano, middle middle) completed the group. They played waltzes, English musicals, and American ragtime as two separate ensembles during lunch and dinner and other shipboard activities.

"I learned to love him that night, and I suddenly felt for him a great reverence to see him standing there sticking to his work while everybody else was raging about. I will never live to forget the work of Phillips for the last awful fifteen minutes."

Racing to his bunk and pulling his life jacket from beneath it, Bride suddenly remembered "how cold the water was." Hoping to keep warm if he could find "anything detached that would float," he pulled on his boots and an extra jacket. Meanwhile, Phillips continued to communicate with the wireless operator on the *Carpathia,* giving details of what was taking place aboard the *Titanic.*

With the doomed vessel about to go under, Phillips made contact with another vessel of the White Star Line. Equipped with a powerful wireless system, the *Olympic* received the message that her sister ship was "sinking by the head and was about all down." She was, however, so far away that her captain decided it would be futile to attempt to reach the site of the shipwreck. With his fellow Marconi operator still at the key, Bride strapped a life belt to Phillips's back. Pausing for an instant, Phillips asked Bride to "see if all the people were off in the boats, or if any boats were left, or how things were."

Near one of the *Titanic*'s immense funnels—fully twenty-four feet in diameter at the base—Bride spotted a collapsible boat that twelve men were trying to put into service. "They were having an awful time," he remembered. "It was the last boat left. I looked at it longingly a few minutes. Then I gave them a hand, and over she went. They all started to scramble in on the boat deck, and I walked back to Phillips. I said the last raft had gone."

At that moment, the voice of Captain Smith boomed: "Men you have done your full duty. You can do no more. Abandon your cabin. Now it's every man for himself. You look out for yourselves. I release you. That's the way of it at this kind of a time. Every man for himself."

Bride scanned the boat deck, now awash with seawater. Phillips refused to leave his post and for ten or fifteen minutes continued to send and receive messages. By that time, water was gushing into the wireless cabin. A burly member of the crew, believed to have been a stoker, slipped into the cabin and from behind tried to pull the life belt from Phillips.

"I suddenly felt a passion not to let that man die a decent sailors' death," Bride admitted. "I wished he might have stretched

When the Carpathia *docked in New York on Thursday night, April 18, 1912, Harold Bride was assisted ashore because his feet had been badly frostbitten.*

rope or walked a plank. I did my duty. I hope I finished him. I don't know. We left him on the cabin floor of the wireless room, and he was not moving."

Incredibly Brave Musicians

As the two wireless operators left their post in search of any kind of flotation device, "From aft came the tunes of the band. It was a rag-time tune, I don't know what. Then there was 'Autumn.' Phillips ran aft, and that was the last I ever saw of him alive."

Returning to the spot where earlier he had seen the collapsible boat, to Bride's surprise the men surrounding it were still futilely trying to push it over the side. He added his strength to theirs just as a large wave rolled up the deck.

"The big wave carried the boat off. I had hold of an oarlock, and I went off with it. The next I knew I was in the boat," Bride recalled. "That was not all. I was in the boat, and the boat was upside down, and I was under it. And I remember realizing that I was wet through, and that whatever happened I must not breathe, for I was under water."

Precisely how he escaped, the wireless operator did not know, but when he "felt a breath of air at last" he found hundreds of men in the water. "The sea was dotted with them, all depending on their lifebelts. I felt I simply had to get away from the ship. She was a beautiful sight then."

Less than a day later, he knew that his estimate of the number of swimmers was only approximate. Column after dreadful column of most major Western newspapers was soon devoted to lists of *Titanic* passengers. More than fifteen hundred names were published, meaning lasting sorrow to relatives of men, women, and children who had gone down with the ship or who quickly froze in the twenty-eight-degree water of the North Atlantic.

According to Bride, "Smoke and sparks were rushing out of her funnel. There must have been an explosion, but we had heard none. We only saw the big stream of sparks. The ship was gradually turning on her nose—just like a duck does that goes down for a dive. I had only one thing on my mind—to get away from the suction. The band was still playing. I guess all of the band went down."

That assumption later proved to be correct; with the melody of "Autumn" floating through the icy air, Bride swam as best he could. "I suppose I was 150 feet away when the *Titanic* on her nose, with her after-quarter sticking straight up in the air, began to settle—slowly," he told the *New York Times* reporter who had come to get his story.

A Hair-breadth Escape

Swimming away from the doomed liner as rapidly as he could, Bride was surprised to feel no undertow as the vessel went down. "I forgot to mention," he later told the *Times* reporter, "that besides the *Olympic* and *Carpathia,* we spoke to some German boat, I don't know which, and told them how we were. We also spoke to the *Baltic.* I remembered those things as I began to figure what ships would be coming towards us."

Soon the twenty-one-year-old realized that he was very cold. He caught a glimpse of a boat and swam toward it with all his strength. He was at the point of exhaustion when "a hand reached out from the boat and pulled me aboard. It was our same collapsible. The same crowd was on it."

There was barely enough room for Bride to lie near the edge of the craft, not caring what might happen next. His legs, wedged between slats, were injured when someone sat upon them. It didn't seem to matter. "It was a terrible sight all around—men swimming and sinking."

With the collapsible boat apparently about to capsize, someone suggested that the men crowded together on it should pray. He inquired about religious backgrounds of his companions and found that the little craft carried at least one Catholic, one Methodist, and one Presbyterian.

"It was decided that the most appropriate prayer for all was the Lord's Prayer. We spoke it over in chorus with the man who first suggested that we pray as the leader." Later, folk aboard "a right-side-up boat," already crowded, somehow managed to pull into it the entire company from the collapsible boat. Lights seen from a distance seemed to Bride to mean that a rescue steamer was near.

"I didn't care what happened. I just lay and gasped when I could and felt the pain in my feet. At last the *Carpathia* was alongside and the people were being taken up a rope ladder. Our boat drew near and one by one the men were taken off of it."

One man was found to be dead as the others began to leave the boat. Bride identified him as Phillips, who presumably had died from exposure and cold. Despite terrible pain in his feet, Bride managed to crawl to the top of the ladder, where he felt hands reaching out for him. "The next I knew a woman was leaning over me in a cabin, and I felt her hand waving back my hair and rubbing my face."

After he managed to accept a swallow of liquor, the Marconi man was hustled into the sick bay. He lay there until darkness was approaching and then was told that the *Carpathia*'s wireless man was getting "queer" and needed help.

"After that," he reported, "I never was out of the wireless room, so I don't know what happened among the passengers. I saw nothing of Mrs. Astor or any of them. I just worked wireless. The splutter never died down."

After having attempted to respond to a few wireless inquiries from newspapers, Bride "shut off the inquiries" and dispatched nothing but personal messages from survivors. Looking back upon those terrible hours, he noted that "I feel I did the [right] thing."

In his opinion, if the *Chester*'s operator had been "decent," he could have worked with him much longer. This man, however, "got terribly" on Bride's nerves "with his insufferable incompetence." He was still sending personal messages when Marconi and the *Times* reporter arrived to ask that he prepare a detailed statement.

After talking at length, he abruptly told his visitors, "An ambulance man is waiting with a stretcher, and I guess I have got to go with him. I hope my legs get better soon."

Pausing reflectively, he added: "The way the band kept playing was a noble thing. I heard it first while we were still working wireless, when there was a ragtime tune for us, and the last I saw of the band, when I was floating out in the sea with my lifebelt on, it was still on deck playing 'Autumn.' How they ever did it I cannot imagine. That and the way Phillips kept sending after the Captain told him his life was his own, and to look out for himself, are two things that stand out in my mind over all the rest."

Bride's lengthy account, published in first-person style, provided the first details of the *Titanic* disaster that went to the general public. He ended his story by saying that he deeply regretted having been forced to leave behind in the *Carpathia*'s wireless room a stack of about one hundred unsent messages from passengers on the ill-fated *Titanic*. Other survivors soon furnished the press with so many accounts of their experiences that the wireless operator dropped out of the news despite the fact that his hair reputedly turned white within a month.

After his dockside interview in New York, Bride never again spoke of the *Titanic,* even to close relatives who did not learn of his exploits until they discovered newspaper clippings in a Bible long afterward. Whether the world knew it or not, he realized that his idea of switching signals from CQD to SOS had been of immeasurable importance.

A decade after the disaster he was found to be living about three hours from London and serving as wireless operator aboard a cross-channel ferry. He then disappeared—apparently deliberately—for half a century. After Bride's death, Walter Lord, author of *A Night to Remember*, tried to trace his later movements but discovered only that at about age seventy-five a man calling himself Harold Bride spent some time in a Glasgow, Scotland, hospital.

2

GUGLIELMO MARCONI

CHAMPION LIFESAVER

ALTHOUGH THERE is no documentation to prove it, Jim Speers, the *New York Times* reporter who boarded the rescue ship *Carpathia* before she docked, owed his interview with Harold S. Bride and his story on the *Titanic*'s sinking to Guglielmo Marconi. Well known to New York authorities, the famous Italian probably insisted that the two men should be permitted to board the vessel despite the No Visitors notices that were posted prominently. Marconi was keenly aware that his operators, most of whom were in their twenties, were paid low wages. Because Marconi's equipment and his operators were central to the *Titanic* story when it made headlines around the world, the great man gave his permission to Bride to sell his account to the newspaper and later did the same thing for Harold T. Cottam, his employee aboard the *Carpathia*.

When the *Titanic* set out on her maiden voyage, hardly anyone in the Western world would have challenged the notion that she was capable of overcoming almost any difficulty encountered in the North Atlantic. John G. "Jack" Phillips and Bride were aboard, not as members of the crew but as employees of the Marconi Company. The physicist-inventor is mentioned incidentally in some reports on the loss of the *Titanic*, but few understand that the sea would likely have claimed all twenty-two hundred victims had not Marconi equipment and operators been aboard. All of the approximately seven hundred persons who survived owed their rescue directly to the man now widely known as "the father of radio."

IN 1898 the Prince of Wales lay ill aboard the royal yacht *Osborne*, and Queen Victoria was in residence at Cowes, only a few miles

Samuel F. B. Morse in the workshop where he invented the telegraph. His code or "telegraphic alphabet" consisted of dots, dashes, and spaces. When he failed to acquire European patents, his code was pirated and modified by eliminating spaces.

NINETEENTH-CENTURY AMERICANS AT WORK

from her son. Since the ruler of the British Empire sometimes herself became ill when aboard a boat, especially a small one, she did not welcome the notion of traveling across the water daily to see her son. Her advisers therefore suggested a novel expedient. A young Italian had previously demonstrated that messages could be sent over some distance without wires. Would it not be well to see if he could transmit medical bulletins from the yacht to the queen's residence?

Within a few days the twenty-four-year-old Marconi had erected his equipment. With the future king of England and the duke of York as interested observers, he tapped upon a key and in Morse code spelled out the message: "The Prince of Wales sends his love to the queen and hopes she is none the worse for being onboard yesterday." Never before had humans achieved ship-to-shore communication by other than visual methods such as flags, lights, and smoke signals.

Every day until his royal host was pronounced recovered, Marconi sent bulletins to the queen. No message conveyed startling or extraordinary news, but each of the approximately 150 reports was published in the London *Times.* Already having received recognition for his work from his fellow scientists, Marconi had become a celebrity.

During his boyhood in Bologna, Marconi had many more advantages than his peers. After studying under a tutor for a number of years, the youth continued his education at the lyceum in Leghorn, where some faculty members were especially inter-

In London, Guglielmo Marconi (right) demonstrated his device to the brother of England's attorney general.

ested in physics. After completing his formal studies, Marconi kept in touch with these teachers.

In 1894 one of them called his attention to the work of German physicist Heinrich R. Hertz. A few years before Hertz's death, the distinguished professor at Bonn had demonstrated the existence of "electric or electromagnetic waves," which for a time were called "Hertzian waves." No one had yet put the scientific breakthrough to practical use, and Marconi became intrigued with the idea of communicating by means of the newly discovered invisible waves.

At first he was most interested in seeing how far Hertzian waves could travel through the air. Experimenting with a variety of homemade devices, he sent a signal from one end of his father's attic to the other. Soon he discovered that a large antenna could pick up signals sent from the far end of the Marconi estate, more than a mile away, to rooms set aside as a laboratory that he shared with silkworms, which were an important source of revenue for the family.

Thoughout the crisis following the collision with the iceberg, Phillips and Bride sent countless calls for help. Above is one of the transcribed messages showing the comingling of the older distress call—CQD—with the new international distress call—SOS. The rest of the transmission noted: "We are sinking fast. Passengers are being put into boats." MGY, which appears at the beginning and end of the message, are the call letters for the Titanic.

The magnetic telegraph invented by Samuel F. B. Morse had been in wide use for several decades. Marconi speculated that by using Hertzian waves he could transmit telegraph messages through the air without using wires. He took the results of his experiments and his unproven theories to the Italian government, but no one showed any interest.

More than a year after he demonstrated that his "wireless" signals could be transmitted over considerable distance, Marconi went to England where he had influential relatives. In February 1896 an Irish cousin helped him to apply for a patent, but it was contested, correctly observing that Marconi had only duplicated the pioneering work of Hertz. Nevertheless, Marconi's cousin helped him to win patents in 1897 and then arranged for several government officials to witness demonstrations of the wireless telegraph. These exhibitions led to the organization of the Wireless Telegraph and Signal Company, Ltd. By 1900 Marconi had succeeded in transmitting messages across 150 miles.

Marconi then set out to send signals across the Atlantic Ocean. He designed and built in Cornwall, England, a transmitter, and at Cape Cod, Massachusetts, the infant American Marconi Company erected a fifty-kilowatt receiving station. In 1901 a message was broadcast from President Theodore Roosevelt to King Edward VII. After wind destroyed the Massachusetts apparatus, the inventor went to Newfoundland with an immense kite that carried an antenna, and on December 12, 1901, communication entered a new era. Incredibly, his airborne antenna caught the signal. At age twenty-seven, the Italian had found a way to send messages across the North Atlantic Ocean without laying eighteen hundred miles of cable.

Transmission of a wireless message across the British Channel earlier in 1899 had marked another giant step in the progress of Marconi. His pioneer transatlantic stations at Clifden, Ireland, and Glace Bay, Nova Scotia, began offering their services to the public on a limited scale in 1907 and then went into "general public service" the following year. Operators who worked in the Canadian maritime province did not dream that within five years wireless radio would make Halifax a nerve center of the Western Hemisphere.

Soon the British Marconi Company constructed and operated stations at Carnarvon, Wales, and New Brunswick, New Jersey. Then the same unit of the Italian's near-global operations erected a station at Marion, Massachusetts, and achieved smooth communication with another station at Stavanger, Norway. Equipment similar to that being used in Norway was being developed for San Francisco and Honolulu when the *Titanic* set out on its first voyage across the Atlantic Ocean.

A few months after having shown that a lightship could be contacted at a distance, Marconi's equipment contacted a Ramsgate lifeboat to come to the aid of a vessel that had run aground. When the lightship was hit by a steamer, her captain signaled for aid by means of wireless. Soon a few farsighted executives began putting wireless systems on their vessels. During century after century in which men took to the sea, little or nothing was known about a vessel from the time it disappeared over the horizon until it reached port. Now it was possible for ships to communicate across

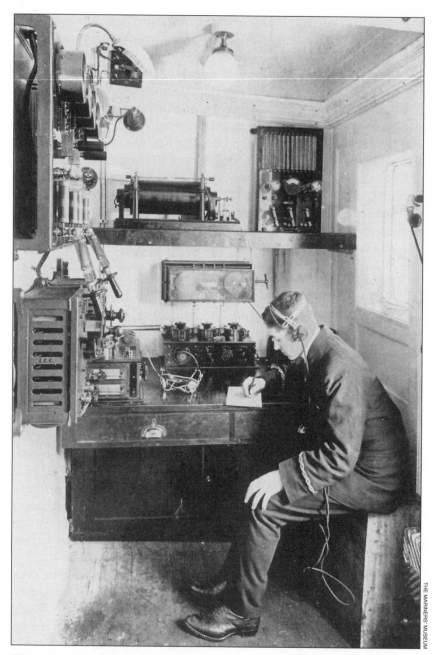

THE MARINERS' MUSEUM

The telegraph room of the Titanic *was not as cramped as that of an Atlantic liner photographed above.* Titanic's *facility was spread over three rooms: one for the dynamo that powered the wireless, one with a bunk, and one used to operate the communications system.*

vast distances with one another on the sea and also maintain contact with stations on land.

Progress was so rapid that within a decade after Marconi received his patents, most passenger ships of any size were using his wireless device. In 1909 the White Star liner *Republic* collided with the Italian vessel *Florida* more than twenty miles from Nantucket. Youthful John Binns, a Marconi employee who was on the *Republic,* called for help just minutes after his vessel was struck. Comparatively undamaged, the little *Florida* packed aboard as many persons as possible, but many were left on the deck of the fast-sinking *Republic*. Responding to the Binns call from a considerable distance, the *Baltic* arrived in time to save about one-third of the fourteen hundred passengers who had been aboard the damaged liner. Marconi and his invention were heralded in the newspapers because Binns's wireless messages had facilitated the saving of lives during a maritime disaster.

In 1909 Marconi also installed his equipment aboard two vessels whose mission was to report the Americas Cup yacht race to the New York newspapers. The success of this venture paved the way for the formation of the American Marconi Company. One year later the Marconi International Marine Communication Company, Ltd., was formed with the goal of providing equipment and operators for ocean liners. Almost certainly influenced by the experience of the *Republic,* when the White Star Line began planning the construction of the mammoth *Olympic*-class liners, an unusually large wireless cabin and accommodations for two operators were included.

IN 1912 Marconi and some of his assistants were called to testify at both the British and American investigations into the *Titanic* disaster. During the British hearings, the inventor was chided for having approved the sale of his operators' experiences to the newspapers. There is no record that he acknowledged this rebuke in any way other than an icy stare directed toward Lord Mersey, who had indicated his indignation at such proceedings.

Had a reporter queried the Italian late in life concerning his most notable achievement, it is unlikely that Marconi would have referred to his role in the drama of the *Titanic*. When it became well known that his wireless had played a unique role in the rescue operations, several reporters besieged his apartment in New York's Holland House. Questioned, he conceded that his wireless did "play a part in the rescue of passengers from the *Titanic*." Newspapers reported that he then added quietly, "That is one of the things radio is for. It has simply done what it was meant to do."

3

BELFAST

BEHEMOTH!

VETERAN WORKMEN at the Harland and Wolff shipyard in Belfast, Ireland, sometimes brought their relatives from the surrounding countryside to see their handiwork. Late in April 1910 a small caravan of country folk visited the shipyard "to see the sight of their lives," as one of the men expressed it. In one wagon a farm woman obediently closed her eyes as soon as she caught a whiff of saltwater and was jolted along for half an hour before she was told to open them. After glimpsing the awesome structure straight ahead, she exclaimed, "Hold your wisht [be quiet]; it's the Behemoth himself!"

Use of the biblical name for a monster was natural at the first sight of the nearly finished RMS *Titanic*. She was sitting near the River Lagan under a gantry 220 feet high, and the tips of the vessel's two masts seemed almost to reach for the sky. Slightly more than one-sixth of a mile in length, the *Titanic* had a navigating bridge 104 feet above her keel, with four enormous funnels, tilted back in rakish fashion, rising more than sixty feet from the boat deck.

"She's a baste [beast]," grinned the carpenter who had arranged the informal inspection trip. "Only thing like 'er in the world is 'er twin sister. I worked better'n two years on the *Olympic*, and nearly as long on this un here."

William James Pirrie of Belfast, who had been created a baron in 1906 and later became a viscount, always believed that his monarch conferred his titles in gratitude for his big thoughts that led to the production of the largest moving things in the world. When Pirrie landed his first job as an apprentice draftsman at the age of fifteen, he did not dream that he would

The White Star Line was the heir to a line of mid-nineteenth-century wooden sailing ships that engaged in profitable trade with Australian immigrants. In 1870 Thomas H. Ismay acquired it and turned to the more lucrative transatlantic passenger traffic— bringing immigrants to the New World and shuttling more affluent passengers between continents. Almost immediately, the White Star Line became known for luxurious accommodations and rapid crossings.

eventually become head of the most famous shipbuilding company in Great Britain.

Long before Pirrie became its controlling chairman, Harland and Wolff entered into an informal partnership with the White Star Line. Provided that the transportation line would buy from no one else, the Belfast firm would build on a cost-plus basis, with a "letter of agreement" in lieu of a contract stipulating a fixed price. Before that arrangement came to an end, Harland and Wolff constructed more than sixty vessels for White Star.

By the time J. Bruce Ismay took over the management of White Star from his father in 1892, the line was a power in the shipping business. Yet Ismay realized that it would take a dramatic move to get an edge on his competitors, which included the Cunard Line. Pirrie was gratified when his young business associate remarked that Harland and Wolff's *Oceanic*, built for the Australian trade and launched in 1871, was lauded on both sides of the Atlantic as "the mother of modern liners." In 1907 Pirrie and Ismay reached a tentative agreement on a grandiose plan.

They reasoned that passengers who were prone to travel frequently between New York, London, and the Continent would prize comfort over speed. The more affluent were less likely to fret over an extra day or even a day and a half. If emphasis were placed on speed, at best White Star could match the Cunard vessels, but that in itself did not promise to attract passengers. Opulence would distinguish the White Star liners from those of its competitors and attract the wealthy.

Since this approach would call for Harland and Wolff to expand and remachine its facilities, the two agreed that it was more cost-effective to plan for three vessels. Pirrie appointed Thomas Andrews, head of his drafting department, to prepare a set of plans for "the biggest thing afloat." In the meantime, Ismay was named to head the International Mercantile Marine holding company assembled by American financier J. Pierpont Morgan.

In midsummer 1908 Ismay met with Pirrie in Belfast, and after two days of discussion that led to some modifications in the plans submitted by Andrews, a general agreement was signed. Before the week ended, Pirrie's general manager, Alexander M. Carlisle, informed his workforce that he could use a few more men immediately and "a lot more in time to come."

Before the year ended, the keel was laid for an immense vessel named the *Olympic*. Three months later, on March 31, 1909, the keel of her sister ship was laid. Meanwhile, the payroll at the shipyard swelled past fourteen thousand men, most of whom worked a standard forty-nine hours a week for wages slightly below ten dollars per week.

When completed, the *Olympic* measured 852.5 feet from bow to stern. Half again as large as the Cunard Line's *Lusitania* and *Mauretania,* she gave her name to a new class of liners that would include at least two more vessels. As was his custom, Ismay went to New York on the *Olympic*'s maiden voyage and made meticulous notes over the ten days he spent aboard ship during her round trip.

Upon returning to his offices in London, Ismay prepared his proposals for modifications that he felt would be appreciated by more affluent travelers. One important change was the enclosure of a promenade—open on the *Olympic*—attached to quarters that soon became known as "millionaire suites." New to the shipping trade, Ismay added the Café Parisian, which had the ambience of a sidewalk café, and replaced many of the portholes with windows.

The names of White Star vessels traditionally ended in "ic." Hence *Titanic,* meaning "colossal" and evoking the gigantic Titans of Greek mythology, seemed appropriate for the second of the three vessels under construction.

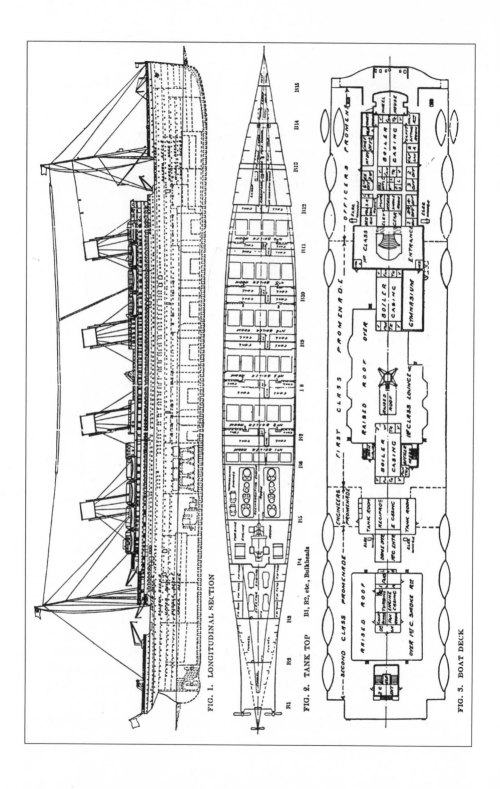

FIG. 1. LONGITUDINAL SECTION

FIG. 2. TANK TOP   B1, B2, etc., Bulkheads

FIG. 3. BOAT DECK

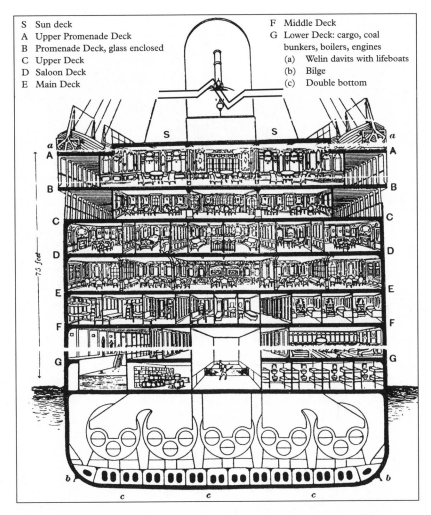

S Sun deck
A Upper Promenade Deck
B Promenade Deck, glass enclosed
C Upper Deck
D Saloon Deck
E Main Deck

F Middle Deck
G Lower Deck: cargo, coal
   bunkers, boilers, engines
(a) Welin davits with lifeboats
(b) Bilge
(c) Double bottom

The Titanic *and her sister ship, the* Olympic, *were the last ships to follow the yacht-inspired shape for which Harland and Wolff were renowned. Apparent in the longitudinal section on the facing page, elegant, unbroken lines carried from the bow to the stern. Four gracefully angled, equally spaced funnels implied a sense of power and proportion. The waterline cross section (middle, facing page) shows the placement of the engines, other machinery, and the six boiler rooms. The promenades on the boat deck (bottom, facing page) were new to transatlantic travel, and the enclosure of the first-class promenade forever distinguished the* Titanic *from the* Olympic. *The transvere sectional above reveals the machinery at the lowest level and such things as the saltwater swimming pool in the lower left corner of G Deck and the squash court amidships.*

LIBRARY OF CONGRESS

In Harland and Wolff's Belfast shipyard, the Titanic *takes shape in slip number three, embraced by a latticework of timber and steel that comprised the largest gantry ever constructed. The gantry allowed workmen to have access to all parts of the ship as it was being built.*

Instead of having two elevators as specified in her plans, when finished the *Titanic* had three elevators for first class and one for second class. A *New York Times* reporter raved that the vessel was "100 feet longer than any other, save the *Olympic,* if set on end would have reached high above the Metropolitan Tower [of New York] as well as the new Woolworth building."

Charles H. Lightoller, who was later named second officer of the new vessel, wrote of her: "It is difficult to convey any idea of the size of a ship like the *Titanic,* when you could actually walk miles along decks and passages, covering different ground all the time. I was thoroughly familiar with pretty well every type of ship afloat, from a battleship and a barge, but it took me fourteen days before I could with confidence find my way from one part of that ship to another by the shortest route."

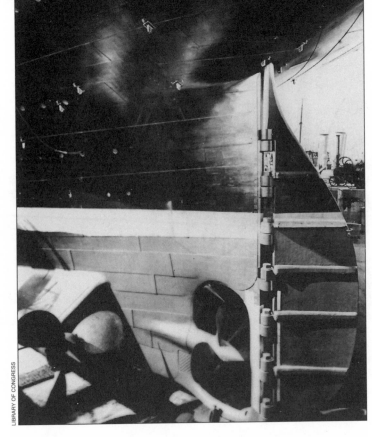

Titanic was a triple-screw liner. Reciprocating engines drove the port and starboard wing screws, and a revolutionary low-pressure turbine turned the center screw. The design was economical and generated little vibration. Together the three engines produced fifty-five thousand horsepower capable of propelling the forty-five-thousand-ton ship at a top speed of twenty-four to twenty-five knots.

At Belfast, Pirrie took the initiative concerning modifications of the ship's machinery. He was delighted to inform *Shipbuilder* magazine that the unfinished *Titanic* was the first vessel in the world to be powered by three screws instead of the conventional two wing screws that were essential to maneuvering and which were turned by thirty-thousand-horsepower engines. The novel third screw, set in the middle, was powered by a low-pressure Parsons turbine that could develop sixteen thousand horsepower.

LIBRARY OF CONGRESS

On May 31, 1911, the Titanic *was launched before an estimated crowd of one hundred thousand. There was no christening, and after a short inspection tour, the ship was guided into the graving dock where her fitting out was completed over the following ten months.*

Originally designed for a passenger load of 1,320 and a crew of just over 900, the *Titanic* received great publicity for her sixteen separate watertight compartments. The heavy doors of these compartments could be closed electrically from the bridge with the touch of a button.

Contrary to many published accounts, White Star never claimed that its most splendid vessel was invulnerable. It was a writer for *Shipbuilder* rather than Pirrie or Ismay who lauded the *Titanic* as "unsinkable" because it could remain afloat even after a number of compartments had been flooded. Once conferred, the title was accepted as accurate by the general public. Other mistakes made by the press had less impact. "The Titanic," said the *Times*, "presented the appearance of a great fifteen-story floating palace." In fact, the gigantic liner had only eight steel decks plus cargo space and a boat deck.

Equipped with sixteen large wooden lifeboats, as required by English statutes, the *Titanic* carried four additional Englehardt boats whose canvas sides caused them to be inaccurately described as "collapsible." In addition, the vessel was equipped with 3,560

One of the passengers from Southampton to Queenstown was Francis M. Browne, a schoolteacher and candidate for the Jesuit priesthood who was also an amateur photographer. From April 10 until he disembarked on April 11, he took an extraordinary series of photographs of life onboard the Titanic. *Above is a view of the* Titanic's *boat deck.*

life jackets—far more than would be needed with a full load of passengers and crew. Her wireless room was a marvel to everyone who saw it. The Marconi equipment was of the 1.5 kilowatt variety, the most powerful available for use aboard ship.

In one respect, the appearance of the forty-five-thousand-ton liner was deceptive, for only three of her funnels took smoke from her furnaces upward. Her fourth funnel, at the stern, was a dummy that Pirrie added "for the sake of appearances." There was nothing fake about her rudder, however; it was more than seventy-five feet high and weighed just over one hundred tons. Having agreed in advance that no expense should be spared to make the *Titanic* the most marvelous product of the twentieth century, the builders' informal slogan was "not simply the biggest, but also the best."

Instead of manually driving her rivets that measured one and a quarter inches in diameter, workmen at Harland and Wolff were taught to use a brand-new pneumatic device that was guaranteed to deliver the pressure at which it was set. Thousands upon thousands of rivets were driven into steel plates so beautifully that only a close-up look revealed their presence.

Decades later, after new technology made it possible to examine the wreck of the *Titanic,* a startling discovery was made. A piece of metal that almost certainly came from the vessel's hull, pierced by three rivet holes, was found lying on the ocean bottom. Metallurgist Ken K. Allen subjected the steel to what he described as "a Charpy test for brittleness" and laboratory analysis of its sulfur content.

To his surprise, Allen found that the metal with which the *Titanic* was clad was unusually high in sulfur and that it included sulfide bodies known as "stringers." Even for the period in which the liner was built, the scientist concluded, the sulfur content of the steel was extremely high. As a result, the metal was unusually brittle and instead of bending under pressure was likely to snap.

There is no evidence that Harland and Wolff saved a few thousand pounds by contracting for substandard steel; the metal that they used probably was not known by them to be brittle. Yet Allen went on record as being sure that the steel sides of the *Titanic* were such that the vessel "would never get out of the yard today." In his opinion, the all-important metal skin of the finest vessel afloat did not bend when the iceberg was hit. Instead, it fractured and in doing so doomed the liner.

Despite the care with which the great liner's name was selected, she was never christened. White Star had abandoned that time-honored ceremony. For the launching of the *Titanic,* an estimated 105,000 men, women, and children assembled in Belfast on May 31, 1911, filling the shipyard to overflowing and spreading along both banks of the river. A few venturesome men even climbed to yards and masts of vessels floating in the harbor for better views. Invited dignitaries, including J. Pierpont Morgan, and a corps of journalists came across the Irish Sea aboard the *Duke of*

The fateful journey begins as the Titanic *departs from Southampton.*

Argyll and were given places of honor when they reached Belfast shortly before 8:00 A.M.

It was shortly after noon, however, before Pirrie completed his lengthy final inspection and nodded for a rocket to be fired. At the signal, ropes at the end of the eight-hundred-foot sliding way were cut and the *Titanic* was released. With more than twenty tons of tallow, soap, and engine oil applied to the ways, the monstrous liner slid smoothly downward into the water.

After the vessel that many an Irishman thought deserved to be called *Behemoth* was beautifully launched, the hotels of Belfast were filled with parties of revelers. Many of them knew that it would take nearly another year to complete the interior of the *Titanic* while she lay in her fitting-out basin. Some of them expressed hope that they could be back in Belfast in 1912 to see "the finest piece of work ever executed by mankind" leave the port city for the customary trials preceding her maiden voyage.

Long before the second vessel of the *Olympic* class was completed, work had begun on a third and final ship. Ismay was confident that the three mightiest vessels afloat would win for White Star the lion's share of the lucrative North Atlantic trade.

Considerable evidence supports the conclusion that the younger sister of the *Titanic* was to be known as the *Gigantic*. This name was shelved, however, in favor of *Britannic* when the *Titanic* experienced disaster one month after she successfully passed her sea trials.

4

SOUTHAMPTON

BON VOYAGE

Soon after noon [on Wednesday, April 10, 1912] the whistles blew for friends to go ashore, the gangways were withdrawn, and the *Titanic* moved slowly down the dock [at Southampton, England], to the accompaniment of last messages and shouted farewells of those on the quay."

Second-class passenger Lawrence Beesley, who had never before crossed the Atlantic, was surprised at the manner in which the mighty vessel got under way. He had expected to hear the hooting of whistles and the cheering of crowds who had come to see off loved ones and friends. Not until several minutes passed did he realize that instead of the expected sounds, everything was "quiet and rather ordinary." An instant later he was abruptly jolted from his reverie.

Suddenly Beesley saw a small group of men whom he presumed to be stokers running full speed along the quay, headed for the gangway "with their kit slung over their shoulders in bundles." A man whose uniform indicated that he was a petty officer stood at the shore end of the gangway and refused to let the latecomers aboard. "They argued, gesticulated, apparently attempting to explain the reasons why they were late," the neophyte traveler remembered. "But he remained obdurate and waved them back with a determined hand, the gangway was dragged back amid their protests, putting a summary ending to their determined efforts to join the *Titanic*."

In Boston a few weeks later, Beesley told entranced listeners: "Those stokers must be thankful men to-day that some circumstance, whether their own lack of punctuality or some unforeseen delay over which they had no control, prevented their being in time to run up that last gangway! They will have told—and will no

THE MARINERS' MUSEUM

On April 10, 1912, the Titanic *departed on its maiden voyage from Southampton. As she approached the entrance to the channel, her immense wake pulled a small American liner, the* New York, *from its moorings. The two ships would have collided but for the quick thinking of a tugboat captain, who threw a line to the* New York, *and the timely actions of the* Titanic's *captain, who ordered the engines "half astern," which pushed the American vessel away.*

doubt tell for years—the story of how their lives were probably saved by being too late to join the *Titanic*."

There's no certainty that Beesley ever learned that the members of the crew who were not permitted to board had been drinking in a nearby tavern. Hence it was their thirst for beer that kept them from tragedy in the North Atlantic.

Beesley clearly did not know that there were a number of last-minute cancellations by well-known people. Evangeline Booth, commander of the Salvation Army in the United States, was due to return to her work there, but she decided to stay at her London desk for a few days longer, then take passage on the Cunard Line's faster *Mauretania*. Robert Bacon, U.S. ambassador to France, had planned to be aboard the *Titanic* with his wife and daughter, but Myron P. Herrick, his successor, failed to arrive on schedule.

Reconciled to a ten-day delay, Bacon canceled his reservation and rebooked their voyage aboard the French liner *France*. William H. Vanderbilt was a no-show, but his valet boarded at the last moment. Identified on passenger lists simply as "manservant," he apparently went down with the ship.

Beesley, a young "science master," was eager for a look at educational methods in the United States. Five weeks after he reached New York aboard the rescue ship *Carpathia*, the British teacher was guest of honor at a Boston luncheon where he spoke about his experiences, not knowing that Robert L. O'Brien, the editor of the *Boston Herald*, was among his listeners. O'Brien immediately asked him "as a matter of public interest" to write his account of the disaster, and he introduced him to some executives at Houghton Mifflin publishing company. Published before the end of the year, his volume was the first book-length account of the disaster at sea by a survivor.

Soon after the rebuffed stokers stalked away, Beesley became aware that "as the *Titanic* moved majestically down the dock, the crowd of friends keeping pace with us along the quay, we came together level with the steamer *New York* lying moored to the side of the dock along with the *Oceanic*." Beesley got the name of the larger vessel wrong; neither did he fully understand what happened next until the incident was interpreted for him by veteran travelers. Sure of his facts when he wrote his book, he explained: "As the bows of our ship came about level with those of the *New York*, there came a series of reports like those of a revolver, and on the quay side of the *New York* snaky coils of thick rope flung themselves high in the air and fell backwards among the crowd. . . . Then, to our amazement the *New York* crept towards us, slowly and stealthily, as if drawn by some invisible force which she was powerless to withstand. . . . On the *New York* there was shouting of orders, sailors running to and fro, paying out ropes and putting mats over the side where it seemed likely we would collide."

The *Vulcan*, a tug that had cast off from the bow of the *Titanic* only a few minutes earlier, raced back at full speed. Once she was made fast to the stern of the *New York*, Beesley wrote, she pulled with all her might but had little effect. To him and numerous other passengers and onlookers from shore it seemed that the sterns of the two liners would hit with tremendous force. That they did not, he explained, was due to quick action aboard his vessel: "An officer directing operations stopped us dead, the suction ceased, and the *New York* with her tug trailing behind moved obliquely down the

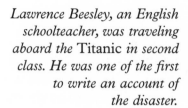

Lawrence Beesley, an English schoolteacher, was traveling aboard the Titanic *in second class. He was one of the first to write an account of the disaster.*

ILLUSTRATED LONDON NEWS

dock, her stern gliding along the side of the *Titanic* some few yards away. It gave an extraordinary impression of the absolute helplessness of a big liner in the absence of any motive power to guide her."

Dubbed simply "unpleasant" by the Englishman who was not superstitious, the incident remained vivid in his memory, partly because of the sights and sounds that he did not understand: "an officer and seamen telephoning and ringing bells, hauling up and down little red and white flags, as danger of collision alternately threatened and diminished."

Second Officer Lightoller, who had survived many an accident at sea, understood the sequence of events better than did Beesley. According to him, "the terrific suction set up in that shallow water" by the movement of the *Titanic* "simply dragged these great liners [*New York* and *Olympic*] away from the wharf." For a minute or two it seemed that nothing could prevent the *New York* from crashing into the stern of the *Titanic*, whose captain reacted to the emergency by giving his mighty liner "a touch ahead on her port engine." This "washed the [*New York*] away, and kept her clear" until other tugs arrived to assist the *Vulcan* in moving her back toward the wharf.

Ismay and the master of the *Titanic*, Capt. Edward J. Smith, had had other difficulties before the ship sailed, especially in finding enough coal for fuel because of a lengthy miners' strike near

At the same time that the Titanic *was sinking, advertisements for the ship's return voyage to Southampton were running in the New York newspapers.*

Southampton. Each of the *Titanic*'s eleven bunkers was designed to hold nearly two hundred tons of coal. Since very little was to be had on land at any price, the company decided to transfer the coal from other ships of the line, even if that meant that the other ships remained at their moorings. Tons were borrowed from the *Oceanic* and *Adriatic,* which caused them to cancel their crossings and transfer their passengers to the *Titanic.* By the time she had almost a full load, the vessel carried thirteen million pounds of coal.

A persistent and undocumented story claims that Ismay and Smith treated the report of a fire in one of the *Titanic*'s bunkers entirely too casually, despite the fact that such fires were common aboard big ships. A striking coal miner from near Southampton might have been blamed for the smoldering blaze, except it seems to have started at Belfast in the starboard bunker of boiler number six. It is believed to have continued to burn for the entire week in which the liner was being provisioned and loaded with cargo at Southampton. If it was not extinguished before the *Titanic* sailed, this fire could account for the fact that numerous survivors were sure they heard a tremendous explosion before she went to the bottom.

This photograph of the promenade on A Deck was taken by Francis M. Browne, and many have identified the lonely figure as that of the Titanic's captain, Edward J. Smith, but the photographer did not not identify him as Smith and it was most unlikely that the captain would be anywhere but on the bridge while a harbor pilot negotiated his ship through the channel.

At Southampton everything seemed picture perfect as the liner "dropped . . . past the shores of the Isle of Wight looking superbly beautiful in new spring foliage." After having exchanged salutes with a White Star tug and passing too far from a group of destroyers to identify the warships, Beesley wrote, "in the calmest weather we made Cherbourg [France] just as it grew dusk." While at this port of call, a few first-class passengers and more than a dozen in second class boarded. Records fail to reveal how many immigrants were directed into steerage, or third-class quarters in the bowels of the monstrous vessel at Cherbourg.

Weighing anchor about 8:30 P.M. and presenting "a most elegant sight as her thousands of electric lights shone brightly through windows and other apertures," the pride of the White

Star Line headed for Queenstown, Ireland. "After a most enjoy-able passage across the [English] Channel, although the wind was almost too cold to allow of sitting out on deck on Thursday morning," the second port of call was reached about noon. A handful of passengers debarked at the Irish port and scores of other passengers came aboard.

Moving into the open sea, the *Titanic* carried slightly more than a full load of passengers. About 315 people were in sumptuous first-class suites and cabins; of these, 198 or 199 survived the ship's collision with an iceberg. Most second-class passengers knew in advance that barriers would prevent their venturing onto the decks on which the rich and famous strolled. Second-class travelers, num-bering about 255, did not fare well when the pride of the White Star Line foundered early the following Monday morning; less than half of them—about 110—reached lifeboats and eventual safety.

Movement from steerage, or third-class quarters was prevented by lockable heavy iron gates. These plain quarters were packed full and long stark dining tables contrasted sharply with those in the first and second class dining areas. White Star records indicated that about 700 men, women, and children were jammed into steerage, but less than 200 of them survived the night of April 14 and the morning of April 15. Class distinctions were never more rigid or frightful than during the hours just before the *Titanic* went to the bottom.

In New York, travel posters had already attracted a substantial number of passengers wanting to go to Great Britain or Europe in *Titanic*'s steerage, although the west-to-east traffic was never as numerous as that of east-to-west.

A few people in the millionaire suites paid fares of about seven hundred dollars a day. On many crossings it was expected that first-class passenger fares would come close to underwriting all of the expenses incurred by the ship's operators, but that amount would not include any profit. Although passengers in steerage were not treated much better than cattle, a full load meant about twenty-five thousand dollars over and above expenses. When fares paid by second-class passengers and freight charges were added, White Star stood to make a handsome profit from each transat-lantic crossing of the *Titanic*.

It is believed that because the passenger list was a bit too long, the *Titanic* sailed with a crew of only 712. Of these, a surprisingly large number came from Southampton. This port was perhaps the most utterly desolate city in the Western world when news of the

This was one of the last photographs taken of the Titanic *as she sailed from Queenstown, a lonely silhouette against the horizon. The ship and two-thirds of the people aboard would never see land again.*

disaster became public, for more than 500 wage earners died at sea, leaving behind grieving and often penniless families.

Valued at $1.25 million, the cargo of the White Star vessel was packed into relatively small spaces that could not be assigned as cabins. With freight charges added to passengers' fares, the maiden voyage of the *Titanic* was considered a financial success before she left port.

During the early afternoon of her first day at sea, the green mountains of Ireland gradually faded in the distance. Beesley and a few others who were on the high seas for the first time recorded their interest in the way in which "the western shores of Great Britain seemed simply to drop into the sea and vanish from sight."

Many of the approximately twenty-two hundred persons aboard remembered that the shouts from shore of "Bon Voyage!" seemed pleasantly appropriate. In just five days, the greatest ocean liner ever built would be anchored in New York Harbor after a passage that would linger delightfully in their memories for the rest of their lives.

5

SMOOTH SAILING

A SEA OF GLASS

THE CLOCKS on the *Titanic* were moved back five hours soon after Ireland disappeared below the horizon. For the remainder of the voyage, all activities would be on New York rather than London time. Captain Smith had earlier decided to keep to what veterans of the North Atlantic called "the outward southern track." This was the standard course taken by ocean liners from mid-January until mid-August—adopted when mariners were under the impression that danger from icebergs ceased about three weeks after Christmas. There seemed to be little or no reason to keep a sharp lookout for ice; during the more than sixty hours after departing from Queenstown, the liner moved with little or no rolling or vibration across "a sea of glass" whose waves were barely discernible from the boat deck.

Except for the music that Mrs. J. J. "Maggie" Brown regarded as "stunning, my dear, simply stunning," Thursday evening was quiet; most persons in first class already had their sea legs, but on the decks below a number of first-time travelers were experiencing dizziness in spite of the fact that the *Titanic* moved with only an occasional perceptible dip.

A few English and European travelers in first class requested tea in their staterooms early Friday morning. Most of them later went into the main dining room for breakfast and were handed menus that offered choices so numerous that passengers in second class would have been overwhelmed: baked apples, fresh fruit, stewed prunes, oats, boiled hominy, puffed rice, fresh herring, findon haddock, smoked salmon, grilled mutton, kidneys and bacon, grilled ham, grilled sausage, lamb collops, vegetable stew, eggs in various styles, sirloin steak and mutton chops to order,

The first-class dining room, of which only a portion is visible here, was the largest such room aboard ship at that time. It was 114 feet long and ran the full width of the hull. Capable of seating five hundred comfortably, it was set with white linen tablecloths, crystal, silver, and chairs decorated with Scottish thistles, English roses, and French fleurs-de-lys.

potatoes, vienna and Graham rolls, soda and Sultana scones, corn bread, buckwheat cakes, black currant conserve, Navarrone honey, and Oxford marmalade.

Far below, members of the huge kitchen and dining staff were busy checking to be sure that the provisions that had been ordered were stored where they could be readily found. Thursday evening's meals had been hastily prepared, but a great many things would be needed on Friday evening. A formal dinner would be served in first and second class. Steerage passengers who had been at table for lunch, would be served tea (supper) while those on the upper decks dined.

By weight, but not in cost, potatoes topped all other commodities listed as "dining provisions." Since they would be used for meals served to passengers of all three classes, 80,000 pounds were aboard. Built-in ice-cooled compartments, too big to be called refrigerators, held about 75,000 pounds of meat and more than

R.M.S. "Titanic"
Restaurant

WHITE STAR TRAINING SHIP "MERSEY"

One of the Titanic's *menus, this one depicted a White Star Line training ship on the cover.*

10,000 pounds of fish. Next in importance in terms of bulk were about 25,000 pounds of poultry and game fowl, 4,000 pounds of salt and dried fish, 7,500 pounds of bacon and ham, and 2,500 pounds of sausage. The ship's stores also included 40,000 eggs and 10,000 pounds of beans, rice, and other dried foods—most of which would be served in steerage. Ten thousand pounds of sugar were packed in sacks. About 9,000 pounds of tomatoes and onions were on hand and shelved separately, as were the 180 boxes of oranges, 50 boxes of lemons, 50 boxes of grapefruit, and 1,000 pounds of hot-house grapes.

Nothing but the best coffee would be served in the elegant dining rooms that were open to first class, but less expensive grinds were shelved for use in second-class dining rooms and steerage. If any passenger had been permitted to enter the coffee room, he would have been overwhelmed by the rich and varied aromas emanating from the 2,200 pounds kept in storage. The ship's galleys also held 1,500 gallons of fresh milk, 600 gallons of condensed milk, 1,200 quarts of fresh cream, 1,750 quarts of ice cream in a wide variety of flavors, 10,000 pounds of cereal, 6,000 pounds of butter, and 1,120 pounds of jams and marmalades. Since the majority of those in first class were Americans, the *Titanic* sailed with only 800 pounds of tea.

Many of the delicacies and staples that were expected to be consumed during five days on the sea were not inventoried by weight. At Southampton, it took several hours to roll 250 barrels of flour into the ship. Nearly 800 bundles of fresh asparagus added considerable bulk, but not as much as 7,000 heads of lettuce. Sweetbreads were counted—1,000—rather than weighed. The "cellars" were well stocked with 20,000 bottles of beer, ale, and stout; 1,500 bottles of wine; 15,000 bottles of mineral water; and 850 bottles of spirits.

White Star liners typically provided a simple bill of fare for third-class passengers. Two compartments on F Deck were designed to accommodate 472 persons; hence many had to wait at each meal. Kosher meat was available for Jewish passengers of all classes, but this was the only standard modification. Food that would be served in steerage at breakfast, dinner, and tea upon a signal from bugler P. W. Fletcher was listed in columns headed by days of the week. Dinner at noon on Friday offered these travelers more choices than their crowded spartan quarters would have suggested: pea soup, lung fish or egg salad, cold beef and pickles, cabbage and boiled potatoes, cabin biscuits or fresh bread, cerealine pudding, and oranges.

Col. Archibald Gracie was a passenger in first class. He was an amateur military historian and had just published a book on one of the lesser known campaigns of the Civil War. Gracie made a habit when crossing to record in a notebook each day's run as posted by the captain or first officer about noon. In the twenty-four hours after leaving Queenstown, he noted with satisfaction that the *Titanic* had covered 385 miles despite the fact that she was far from getting up full steam.

Another American in first class, Maj. Archibald Butt, possessed an international reputation. Currently, he was a military aide to President William Howard Taft, but previously he had been an adventurer, news correspondent, novelist, and diplomat. He was affable and gracious in his manner, which allowed him to be comfortable around royalty as well as commoners. A servant in the White House once described him, "There goes the man that's the highest with the mighty and the lowest with the lowly of any man in this city."

During a quick tour of the vessel, Butt wanted a look at the wireless cabin and was cordially invited to come inside. Unlike many in first class, he did not go back and forth between the United States and Europe with the seasons, but he knew his way around.

"No," he said in reply to a query from the senior Marconi operator, Jack Phillips, "I don't have a message to send today."

The ship's two operators—Phillips and Bride—worked twelve-hour shifts and offered around-the-clock wireless service. Most nights allowed them a few extra hours of sleep when wireless traffic slowed.

One of the hallmarks of the White Star Line was its insistence on providing the best for its passengers. No doubt Vinolia Otto Toilet Soap had hoped to make many repeat customers of the passengers of the Titanic.

Henry Wilde had served as chief officer with Captain Smith aboard the Olympic, *but Smith found that another man had been given that position aboard the* Titanic. *Just prior to departure, Smith requested that Wilde be transferred to the* Titanic. *When this was approved, all ship's officers were bumped down a rank and second officer David Blair was left behind as a result.*

Butt knew the routine as there was an inquiry office on the starboard side of the first-class entrance nearest the bow. Passengers wishing to send a message wrote it out and paid about $2.50 for the first ten words and a surcharge for the rest. The office was linked with the wireless room by two-way pneumatic tubes. Outgoing messages shot rapidly to a receptacle near the elbow of the Marconi operator, who transmitted them as soon as possible. "Passenger traffic," as this flow of words was called, took precedence over nearly everything else. When an incoming message for a passenger was received, it traveled by tube to the inquiry office, where it was handed to a bell boy who searched until he found the person for whom it was intended.

Gracie, Butt, and their fellow travelers in first class went into the 532-seat dining room saloon on D Deck soon after noon on Friday for their first luncheon; waiters had apologized profusely that Thursday's meals were makeshift only. Five courses were on the Friday noon menu, with numerous options from the grill and the buffet.

After lunch, some of the men who knew that a drill was scheduled wandered in the direction of the master fire station. Numerous small pneumatic tubes under a glass-fronted case enabled the

ILLUSTRATED LONDON NEWS

Years before, someone had asked Wallace Hartley bandmaster of the Titanic *orchestra, what he would do if he found himself on the deck of a sinking ship. "I would gather the band together and begin playing," he replied. In the early hours of April 15 he did just that. As the lifeboats were being loaded, the band played a set of lively ragtime tunes to dispel the sense of panic. Throughout the crisis the music varied between ragtime, customary dance tunes, and fashionable waltzes.*

shift chief to communicate almost instantly with secondary fire stations. At each of these, hoses were attached to hydrants so that they could always be at the ready. Every officer knew that the *Titanic* carried the latest and best firefighting equipment.

A handful of sailors were concerned about the disappearance of binoculars normally used by the lookouts posted in the crow's nest. The White Star Line hired men specifically for the position of lookout rather than rotating deckhands to the observation point, and so the binoculars were considered invaluable for the men to do their job. The glasses were aboard, but at the time no one onboard knew where.

A last-minute reshuffling of the officers aboard ship had left the officer in charge of the binoculars in Southampton. Second Officer David Blair had been bumped from the ship when Chief Officer William Murdoch had been replaced by Henry Wilde, who had more experience with White Star's larger vessels. Murdoch was made first officer, which bumped Charles H. Lightoller to second officer. Prior to his leaving the vessel, Blair had ordered the binoculars brought from the crow's nest and then placed them in a locker in his cabin. The shuffling of officers occurred in the hours just prior to *Titanic*'s departure, and Blair either forgot to inform

Lightoller of the binoculars in his cabin or forgot about the binoculars entirely.

Informed of the matter, First Officer Murdoch took a quick look around his quarters but, as he had expected, came up empty-handed. Chief Officer Wilde casually informed George Symons, one of the lookouts, that "the matter of the binoculars is in hand." Apparently he considered it to be of no importance. Thus no powerful glass was available for the men serving as lookouts on the fateful night ahead.

Each day an elaborate inspection of the ship was conducted under the supervision of Captain Smith. Wearing his most splendid uniform, the ship's captain proceeded from the bridge to the boiler rooms. The formal tour was perfunctory, and few passengers in first class did more than pause briefly to watch as Smith and his subordinates moved about. Seasoned travelers knew that a careful inspection of the *Titanic* would take days, not simply the better part of an hour.

Lawrence Beesley found Saturday to be very much like the previous two days. His published account dismissed this period with the comment, "There is very little to relate." The science teacher spent an hour or two trying to analyze the gentle movements of the liner and tentatively decided that some of them may have been due "to the angle at which our direction to New York cuts the general set of the Gulf Stream." He then interested himself in the actions of a steerage passenger whose name he did not learn. Turning his back upon a "most uproarious skipping game of the mixed-double type" then in progress at his level, the third-class passenger climbed laboriously to the second-class deck. There he leaned over an iron fence and talked at length with a woman whom Beesley assumed to be the man's wife. The fellow's breakfast of cereal, kippers, boiled eggs, bread, marmalade, and tea must have given him abundant energy, Beesley decided.

In the mail room the clerks knew that they had only three days to complete their work. On April 17 the *New York Times* echoed a verdict that Gracie stressed in his account of the tragedy. "The Titanic carried 3,423 sacks of mail," reported the newspaper, "according to advice received at the General Post Office here." It was estimated that these held about half a million letters, not counting registered pieces that filled another 200 sacks. Three Americans and two Englishmen served as clerks in the Sea Post Office. Gracie went to the trouble of jotting down their names:

The third-class dining room carried some traces of the craftsmanship and meticulous care evident in first-class accommodations. In many ways steerage passengers ate better food aboard ship than they had ever had at home, and on the Titanic *there was plenty for everyone.*

John S. Marsh, William L. Gwynn, Oscar S. Woody, Iago Smith, and E. D. Williamson. In New York the assistant superintendent of foreign mail, Edwin Sands, told reporters on the Saturday after the disaster that he considered it "just possible" that at least one of the five was saved; his hopes soon proved to be futile.

By Saturday nearly everyone in first class had been present at one or more musicals presented by the ship's eight-man band. Their leader, Wallace Hartley, was a native of Lancashire who had made a number of crossings. Following instructions from Ismay, Hartley prepared a list of 120 overtures, operatic selections, waltzes, suites, and fantasies that he considered likely to please the passengers. This was printed only after the band had rehearsed the numbers to perfection, and then it was distributed to the passengers so they could make requests. Such pieces as "Beautiful Spring" and "Vision of Salome" proved to be favorites.

At midmorning on Saturday, Chief Engineer Joseph Bell reported to the bridge that the ten-day-old fire in boiler room number six had been extinguished. Leading stoker Frederick Barrett, aided by a dozen firemen, got the better of the blaze by removing all of the coal from the room. Watertight bulkhead number five, which was red hot for a period, was a bit warped but otherwise seemed to be in good condition, Bell said.

Second-class passengers enjoyed a delightful luncheon on the fourth day out of Southampton. A menu especially printed for the occasion offered them pea soup, spaghetti au gratin, corned beef or vegetable dumplings or roast mutton, cold baked jacket potatoes, cheese, biscuits, coffee, and a variety of sweets.

Although the passengers in steerage, who did not fare so well that day, knew that those in first class were feasting, there were few audible complaints. Many of the immigrants spoke no English and were accustomed to simple fare. Some were openly joyful at the prospect of soon reaching the land of opportunity to which numerous relatives and friends had gone earlier. Many a family in this category owned nothing except the clothes on their backs; they had sold everything else they had to get passage money.

Humming through the still dark Saturday night so smoothly that a glass of water on a table showed little or no visible movement, the *Titanic* had not yet achieved full speed but was approaching it. Runs were measured from noon to noon before being posted for the information of passengers. In the period that ended at noon on Friday, the ship's 386 miles seemed a snail's pace compared to the 519 miles covered on Saturday and the 546 miles covered by midday Sunday. The *Titanic* was on pace for a record-making run for ocean liners.

Ismay was pleased with the news and discussed with the captain the likelihood of *Titanic*'s bettering the best time of the *Olympic*. In addition to that, there would be plenty of publicity if the ship reached dock ahead of its scheduled arrival and in time for Wednesday's newspapers to cover the story of the newest vessel in the White Star Line as a picture of luxury and speed.

6

DAY FIVE

BEST CROSSING EVER

MANY OF those in first class were more leisurely than usual on Sunday morning, April 14. The majority would be attending divine services at 11:00 in the dining saloon. Despite the fact that the White Star Line had done away with the quasi-religious ceremony of christening its liners, the company took the Sabbath seriously. Captain Smith, following his long-standing custom, led the service himself and used a prayer book printed especially for White Star rather than the Book of Common Prayer.

Around 9:30 Smith received from the wireless room a message from the eastbound *Caronia*, a Cunard liner. It was routine for liners to exchange information regarding weather and sea conditions, and the *Caronia* had encountered ice in several forms—bergs, growlers, and field ice—and gave its position. Icebergs were by definition huge; growlers were comparatively small segments that had broken off icebergs; and field ice was made up of chunks large enough to bear the weight of a man. Busy selecting hymns for the morning's service, Smith scanned the wireless and then posted it for the information of his officers.

Some men and women on the upper decks chose not to dress for breakfast, and others had a leisurely meal before gathering in the saloon's reception room to await the worship service. Someone commented that although she had made many crossings and hoped to make many more, this was "the best ever" because of the luxurious way in which special facilities for first class had been fitted out.

At least a dozen persons were within range of her soft, cultivated voice. When she spoke, virtually everyone who heard her nodded in agreement. A gentleman, possibly Philadelphia industrialist

William Carter, said that he had been in the heated saltwater bathing pool "at least twice every day since we sailed." Colonel Gracie, who had visited the six-foot pool less frequently, opined that even the finest of the hot springs "do not hold a candle to warm seawater."

As the conversation continued and ebbed through the room, swirling over two men intent upon their chess game, several of the *Titanic*'s features were especially lauded. A Bostonian voiced appreciation for the fact that animals were fed and watered regularly "instead of being shoved into a cage and forgotten until in sight of New York harbor." Although he reportedly did not join in the conversation, the owner of what some fellow passengers described as "half of downtown New York" nodded agreement. Even though he was on a delayed honeymoon, John Jacob Astor would not have thought of making a crossing without his blooded Airedale.

Someone gushed that she had never before been aboard a liner equipped with a Turkish bath, and a fellow traveler who had tried its amenities interrupted to stress that it was unique—the only one of its kind aboard ship. Although the library was finished in mahogany and studded with fluted white columns, the beautiful room furnished with armchairs, lounges, and writing tables was not mentioned. Harry Widener of Philadelphia noticed the omission but did not call attention to it.

Charles M. Hays, president of Canada's Grand Trunk Railway, waxed enthusiastic about the gymnasium. Equipped with an electric horse and an electric camel in addition to such standard gear as weight lifting and rowing devices, except for the smoking room, it may have been the most heavily used special feature of the finest ocean liner ever launched. No one mentioned the private promenades alongside a few suites reserved for persons who thought nothing of paying more than four thousand dollars to occupy one of them for a few days.

Nearly half of those who were waiting for Captain Smith's arrival drifted away during a lull in the conversation. Most of them went to the deck to take in the invigorating fresh air. Meanwhile, their maids and valets, who were expected to occupy rows of chairs at the back of the saloon, hurried to complete their chores so that they would not be late for the service.

Smith, who had led many services, had long ago learned that his passengers liked to hear their favorite hymns. When he

THE MARINERS' MUSEUM

Among the special amenities aboard ship was the saltwater swimming pool on F Deck. It adjoined the Turkish baths and electric baths with their state-of-the-art steam rooms, hot rooms, temperate rooms, cooling rooms, and shampooing rooms.

concluded what he called "the ritual," the master of the liner invited suggestions for hymns, but he kept his eye on his watch. When the minute hand had crept past eleven o'clock, he announced, "The first stanza of just one more, ladies and gentlemen. What shall it be?"

Nodding in response to three or four requests, he announced, "Let us raise our voices in praise by using a few lines of the splendid old hymn 'O God, Our Help in Ages Past.'" Following the benediction, passengers were on their own until they returned to the saloon for an elegant luncheon. Beesley and his fellow travelers in second class commented that the Sunday allowed the White Star owners to "provide us with a few extras." In steerage, there was no deviation from the usual fare.

Precisely at noon, a test of the liner's whistles showed them to be in perfect working order. So were the pneumatic tubes that

THE MARINERS' MUSEUM

This area was known as the cooling room and provided passengers with a quiet area apart from the Turkish baths. No expense was spared in the room's luxurious appointments.

linked the bridge with the engine rooms far below. Following White Star procedure, Smith and his chief subordinates took out sextants to determine the precise position the *Titanic* had reached. The ship's latitude and longitude were entered into her log and soon posted in the smoking room along with a notation of the distance covered during the last twenty-four hours.

Glancing into a few compartments in the ship's hold, seamen noted no shifting of cargo. On numerous vessels—including the Cunard Line's fast and highly touted *Lusitania* and *Mauretania*—the movements of the sea that were often felt by the passengers caused cargo to shift enough to affect navigation. Aboard the smooth-as-silk *Titanic*, however, even before they were informed of the results of the inspection, every veteran seaman would have sworn that each crate, barrel, sack, and cask was still where it had been placed by the stevedores.

In the wireless room, malfunctioning equipment had kept Phillips and Bride off the air for hours and created a tremendous backlog of messages to transmit. Most of these had nothing important to say; their senders simply wanted friends and relatives to know that they were being remembered from the floating palace about which there had been so much publicity during the past few months.

Stipulated by White Star officials as part of the Sunday routine, a lifeboat drill was canceled because there was "too much wind this morning," according to the captain. He hardly needed to find an excuse for his decision, for Ismay knew quite well that most of his captains had so much confidence in their vessels that lifeboat drills were seldom held.

Even had there been a drill, it would have had little effect on later events. According to the Board of Trade, the drill required a ship's officer to supervise a picked crew to uncover a designated lifeboat on each side of the ship, swing it over the side, and climb aboard. Some fastidious officers required the crew to check the lifeboats' oars, mast, sail, and rigging, but most overlooked this checklist. Afterward, the crew climbed out of the lifeboat, swung it back into its original position, replaced the cover, and returned to their duties. On the *Titanic* only crew members were assigned to specific lifeboat stations; the passengers had no assignment of any kind.

Just after 1:30 P.M. Phillips took a call from the liner *Baltic*. Bound for Liverpool out of New York, the ship passed along word received from the Greek cargo vessel *Athinia* that large quantities of field ice and many bergs had been encountered not far north of the path of the *Titanic*. He sent it to Captain Smith who showed it to Ismay who pocketed it. The German liner *Amerika* followed quickly with a message regarding the locations of two icebergs it had just passed. The message was addressed to the U.S. Hydrographic Office, but the *Amerika*'s equipment was weaker than the *Titanic*'s, and the operator asked Phillips to pass on the message. Phillips also kept a copy for his captain.

Days later, Bride, the junior wireless operator, admitted that the message from the *Amerika* should have been sent to the bridge immediately. Soon he learned that the son and daughter-in-law of department store magnate and *Titanic* passenger Isidor Straus were returning home on the German liner. Phillips seems to have considered the later message a repetition of information transmitted by the *Baltic,* which he had relayed to the bridge at the first opportunity and had ended up in Ismay's pocket. Ismay apparently forgot about it. As a result, messages about ice were scattered over the ship, and no one had plotted the ice positions other than the midmorning message from the *Caronia.* Had the information been coordinated, it would have shown a seventy-five-mile band of ice in *Titanic's* path. To further complicate matters, the wireless malfunctioned at midafternoon, and Phillips did not finish his repairs until just after 7:00 P.M.

Passengers strolled their respective decks on "a radiantly beautiful Sunday afternoon during which the seas continued to be exceptionally smooth." About 5:00 P.M., however, some of them returned to their quarters shivering noticeably because there had been a sudden drop in temperature from the brisk but pleasant forty-four or forty-five degrees that prevailed when they went on deck.

First- and second-class passengers began dressing for dinner and those in steerage anticipated the ragout of beef scheduled for their tea. On the bridge Smith instructed the helmsman to alter course slightly to keep the vessel on the established southward track. This was not an unusual adjustment, yet some seamen later said that when they noticed the turn, they decided that Smith had decided "to play it safe and keep well south of floating ice."

Nearly two hours later, First Officer William Murdoch took steps designed to shield the eyes of the lookouts from the lights of the liner. Every old salt knew that ice was hard to see on a calm dark night. Anything that cut visibility of the watch in the crow's nest would make it more difficult to spot ice at a distance. Before all offending lights had been turned off or shielded, in the ever-busy wireless cabin, the Leyland liner *Californian* called to warn the *Titanic* of "three large bergs five miles southward of us" and gave their position as 42.3 N, 49.9 W. Bride saw to it that this message went to a ship's officer, but he was unable later to remember the identity of the man who accepted it from him. The ice was now fifty miles ahead of the *Titanic.*

Captain Smith probably never saw the warning sent from the *Californian* because after dinner he was invited to a special reception in his honor regarding his retirement once *Titanic* arrived in New York. The reception was hosted by George D. Widener of

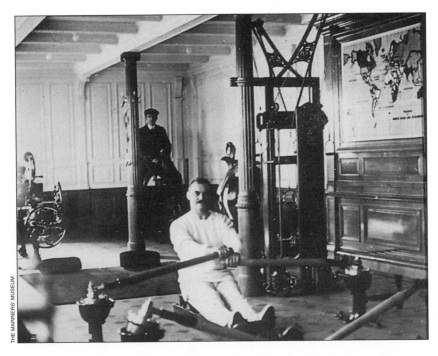

THE MARINERS' MUSEUM

The gymnasium was photographed by Francis M. Browne, and he identified the man in the white flannels as T. W. McCawley, the ship's thirty-four-year-old "physical educator." A passenger recalled that McCawley was strict with most of the travelers but tenderhearted with children. The room had the latest equipment, and the walls were painted pine with oak wainscotting. The illuminated glass map on the right showed the routes of the White Star's liners. The man in the rear corner is William Parr, an electrician and one of the shipbuilder's representatives making sure that all Titanic's *appointments worked properly. The electric camel on which he is sitting received a thorough workout from the people who toured the ship in Southampton, and Parr likely was confirming that the exercise machine was still functional. Both men were lost at sea.*

Philadelphia—whose fortune came from control of the city's transit systems—and held in the à la carte restaurant. Also attending were the Wideners' son Harry, who had a reputation as a collector of rare books, Maj. Archibald Butt, the John B. Thayers, and the William Carters.

ARCHIVE PHOTO

Francis M. Browne also captured this image of six-year-old Robert Douglas Spedden playing with a top at the aft end of A Deck. Spedden's father, Frederic, closest to him, looks on. They were from Tuxedo Park, New York, and both survived the sinking with Mrs. Spedden and two servants. Sadly, three years later, Douglas was killed in an auto accident in Maine. His father drowned in 1947 when he suffered a heart attack in a swimming pool in Florida.

In the dining saloon, an elegant eleven-course dinner was served. After having chosen from a variety of entrées, passengers feasted on lamb with mint sauce, roast duckling with apple sauce, sirloin of beef with château potatoes, or filets mignon prepared in the special fashion known as "Lili."

Had anyone spent a few minutes with the members of each shipboard class, he could have readily distinguished them by their conversation at the table. In first class, there was much talk about soon having to repack valises and other containers; many were glad to be nearing home but at the same time confessed that they would probably find themselves a bit reluctant to leave their floating palace.

Lawrence Beesley and a few others in second class with whom he had become acquainted observed they would not bother to begin packing their limited clothing until New York was in sight. Busy drafting a list of cities he hoped to visit during his stay in America, the teacher did not enter into a prolonged conversation. After dinner he joined about one hundred other passengers from second class in their dining saloon for the traditional hymn singing of a Sunday evening. All of the hymns were requested by the passengers, and the Reverend Earnest Carter, an Anglican priest, delayed the singing for only as long as it took him to recall something of the hymn writer or the history of the hymn. Beesley noticed that several of the hymns chosen dealt with the dangers of traveling on the sea.

In steerage, there were no expressions of regret that they would soon leave the *Titanic*. Conversing in French, Spanish, and German, adults tried to quiet small children while expressing eager optimism that life in the New World would prove to be much better than it had been in the Old World. These folk had been given the privilege of "going up the ship" only once during the voyage—at the time of the Sunday morning worship service. Those who attended were surprised to find that members of the ship's band provided music to accompany the singing of hymns. The eyes of many of them danced with eagerness as they talked of reaching shore and starting new lives.

Shortly after 9:00 P.M. Captain Smith excused himself from the Widener reception to tend to the ship. The men gravitated toward the smoking lounge while the wives excused themselves and retired. Frank D. Millet and Arthur Ryerson had been in the smoking room for some time when the men from the Widener reception joined them. The ladies drifted in and out of the parlors. Still wearing the formal dress they had donned for dinner, Archibald Gracie, James Clinch Smith, and Edward A. Kent sought out their favorite haunt, the Palm Room, and sipped coffee for nearly an hour while listening to the band.

Many passengers retired early. It had been a pleasant day, but the temperature had fallen dramatically since sunset. Very few ventured on deck in the cold weather. The ship's crew was taking steps to see that the fresh water supply would not freeze overnight. The captain retrieved the *Baltic*'s message concerning ice on the water from Ismay and posted it on the bridge. Once he himself was on the bridge, Smith stopped to talk with his second officer as they took their positions and faced the cold night.

7

THE COLLISION

BLUE ICE

BY ALL reports Sunday evening was clear and calm, but neither the captain nor his second officer was pleased. Smith commented on the cold, and Lightoller responded, "Yes sir, it's very cold. In fact it's only one degree above freezing."

"There is not much wind," Captain Smith added.

"No," Lightoller answered. "It's a flat calm, as a matter of fact."

The second officer went on to say that a breeze would give the water a chop that might make it easier to spot any ice as the water washed against the base of a berg or a growler. Smith commented that he was sure the visibility was sufficient to spot a "blue" berg, that is, an iceberg that had overturned. Shortly after 9:30 P.M. Smith turned the *Titanic* over to Lightoller and said, "If it becomes at all doubtful, let me know at once."

Lightoller finished his watch at 10:00 P.M. and was relieved by First Officer Murdoch. The second officer reported on the dropping temperature, precautions being taken to keep the ship's water supply from freezing, special instructions for the lookouts, and the captain's orders to be awakened "if it becomes at all doubtful." Lightoller then went to his cabin, seeking the warmth of his bed.

Writing later, Lightoller recalled that the sea had been like glass for hours. Since the night was clear, he was confident that even a tiny iceberg, or growler, would be detected at a distance of a mile or a mile and a half. Both he and Smith knew that "there had been an extremely mild winter in the Arctic, owing to which, ice from the ice cap and glaciers had broken away in phenomenal quantities."

The second officer also remembered that official reports, which had been routinely sent to the masters of liners, had noted that "never before or since has there been known to be such quantities of icebergs, growlers, field ice and float ice, stretching down with the Labrador current." During his fifteen years on the Atlantic, part of which was spent on sailing vessels near the Antarctic, "I had certainly never seen anything like [the ice in 1912]." Lightoller added: "In ordinary circumstances the cold current carrying the icebergs south strikes the warm current flowing to the northeast and under-runs it—that is to say the cold current goes under the warm current, on the same principle that warm water always rises. The effect of this is to melt the iceberg around the water line. It soon 'calves,' or breaks up into smaller pieces, which again break up, continuing to float in the warm surface current for a short time, until completely melted."

Unfortunately for the *Titanic*, early spring in 1912 was far from ordinary. A number of huge icebergs, exposed to the sun, melted until they toppled over and reversed their position in the sea. For several days after coming to the surface, the ice that had been underwater was especially difficult to see at night because the portion now exposed appeared to be dark blue in color.

Lightoller was convinced that it was one of these blue bergs that lookout Frederick Fleet spotted around 11:40 P.M. without initially being sure of what it was. Having no binoculars and hence forced to rely on his eyes alone, Fleet did not see the immense mass of ice until it loomed a few hundred yards ahead. He instantly rang the warning bell three times to warn the bridge, "Object directly ahead." By this time Fleet and his partner, Reginald Lee, realized that the iceberg toward which the ship was steaming only slightly a bit below full speed loomed almost as high as their perch, which was fifty feet above the forecastle deck.

In addition to the bell, Fleet grabbed the telephone in the box on the mast behind him. The bridge answered almost immediately.

"Iceberg right ahead," Fleet said.

"Thank you," Sixth Officer James Moody responded and then repeated the words to First Officer Murdoch.

"Hard a-starboard!" Murdoch ordered the helmsman and then stepped over to the bronze engine room telegraph and rang for full speed astern for both engines. All three men anxiously watched the bow to see if it cleared the looming iceberg before them.

Lookouts Fleet and Lee braced themselves for collision and then breathed a sigh of relief when the bow turned away at the last possible second. While passing the berg large chunks of ice fell to the foredeck and into the well deck, and both men saw why the

Capt. Edward J. Smith was one of the most respected commercial line captains on the Atlantic. Known and addressed as E. J. by both passengers and crew, Smith emanated a reassuring combination of authority, confidence, and good humor. He was so popular among the passengers who regularly crossed the Atlantic that they even asked for him by name when booking their tickets. For this reason, White Star usually placed Smith at the helm of most of its new ships for their maiden voyages.

berg had been so hard to see. It was a blue berg, having recently overturned, still darkened with seawater.

Lightoller was conscious of the fact the vessel veered slightly to port, but was barely conscious that this was due to a collision.

On the bridge Murdoch reached for the switches to close the watertight doors to the boiler rooms and the engine room then he stepped to the starboard bridge wing and watched the berg as the ship passed by. He was so close, he thought he would touch it if he held out his hand.

Deep within the hull of the *Titanic* the watertight doors closed. The bridge crew concurred that less than thirty seconds elapsed between Fleet's warning and their actions taken to make sure that the ship would not be badly damaged. No one knew that the iceberg's huge protruding "knee," or spur, more than ten feet below the surface of the water had scraped against the side of their vessel for about three hundred feet. Far below, however, icy saltwater gushed into three holds and two engine rooms.

Captain Smith was on the bridge just seconds after the impact. Imperturbably he asked, "Mr. Murdoch, what was that?"

This is most likely the iceberg with which the Titanic *collided. It was photographed on the morning of April 15, 1912, by the chief steward of the German liner* Prinze Adelbert, *a few miles south of* Titanic's *last position. The steward had not yet heard of the sinking; he had seen a smear of red paint along the base of the ice, indicating that it had collided with a ship during the previous twelve hours.*

"An iceberg, Captain," the first officer reported. "I ordered hard-a-starboard and rang for full speed astern. I was going to hard-a-port around it, but it was just too close."

Finding that the watertight doors had been closed as well, the captain ordered all engines stopped. Just then Fourth Officer Joseph Boxhall appeared on the bridge. All three men stepped out onto the starboard bridge wing and tried to spot the iceberg. Returning to the bridge, Smith dispatched Boxhall to the liner's depths to inspect for damage. Authorized by Smith to take whatever steps seemed necessary, he had the engines stopped entirely.

The vibrations caused by stopping her engines awakened more passengers than had the liner's brush with the iceberg. Beesley was reading when he noticed what seemed to him to be "an extra heave of the engines and a more than usually obvious dancing motion of the mattress" on which he sat. Reflecting about this incident afterward, he was sure that there was "nothing more than that—no sound of a crash or of anything else: no sense of shock, no jar that felt like one heavy body meeting another."

At the time, he concluded that Captain Smith "must have still further increased the speed." A few hours afterward he realized that "all this time the *Titanic* was being cut open by the iceberg and water was pouring in her side, and yet no evidence that would indicate such a disaster had been presented to us. It fills me with astonishment now to think of it."

In the smoking room the slight change in the feel of the liner was noticed, but men sitting about a table did not interrupt their card game. A few men in first class walked to the glass-enclosed A Deck and quizzed one another on what might be happening. Archibald Gracie, who had gone to bed much earlier than usual, woke up with a start. Although he was "feeling rather absurd for not remaining in the cabin," he headed for the deck. At least two of his after-dinner companions that evening arrived there ahead of him. Hugh Woolner, son of an English sculptor whose works were in Westminster Abbey, was puzzled about what had taken place. So was H. Bjornstrom Steffanson, a lieutenant in the Swedish army.

Clinch Smith, with whom Gracie was better acquainted, must have been one of the first to reach the deck. As the others stood about chatting, he approached them and announced that the liner had hit an iceberg. When the faces of several of the men showed skepticism, Smith opened his hand to reveal "some ice, flat like a watch." To Gracie, without cracking a smile, he suggested that the retired military officer "might take it home for a souvenir."

A few minutes later a steward who was scurrying past the little knot of curious passengers paused long enough to inform them that the mail room was beginning to flood, but the postal clerks were still at their desks. Simultaneously, Smith and Gracie noticed what they later described as "a list on the floor of the companionway." They said nothing about this matter to others, since a few ladies had left their cabins by that time and they did not wish to alarm them.

First-class passenger Martha E. Stevenson later claimed that "a terrible jar with ripping and cutting noises that lasted for several minutes" woke her up. It reminded her of an April morning six years previously when she was lying in a bed and experienced a similar jolt in San Francisco as the city seemed to fall apart.

Once it became known that an enormous mass of ice really had been hit, a wealthy gentleman from one of the millionaire

For decades it was believed that the iceberg had ripped a lengthy opening along Titanic*'s hull. Only recently was it learned that the collision had buckled the plates rather than ripped them open.*

suites joked that "the iceberg must have scratched off some of this grand lady's new paint, and the captain doesn't want to proceed until the damage has been concealed by a new layer of paint."

When word that the *Titanic* had been lost reached the U.S. mainland, a number of experts offered explanations of the disaster. Capt. Charles A. McAllister, engineer in chief of the Revenue Cutter Service, explained to a *New York Times* correspondent:

> The impact of the Titanic against the iceberg was probably equivalent to the simultaneous firing of 30 twelve-inch projectiles, or the concentrated fire of three such dreadnoughts as the Florida. The fire of 10 twelve-inch guns such as the Florida carries is sufficient to put any battleship afloat out of business, if the projectiles should strike simultaneously. The force of the Titanic striking the iceberg must have been approximately 1,000,000 tons, equivalent to her being struck

by thirty such projectiles. It is a wonder in the light of such a comparison that she floated so long. It is inconceivable that the ingenuity of man can ever devise a floating structure to withstand such a terrific collision.

Also in Washington, Capt. Charles W. Dyson of the Bureau of Steam Engineering of the U.S. Navy talked with a different *Times* correspondent. Having the advantage of holding a set of plans of the *Titanic,* he had studied them carefully before rendering his opinion that "the injury done to the ship was very much greater than any indication yet received in the few meagre dispatches about the disaster." He then went into considerable detail about his theory:

> From the collision bulkhead a long passage way ran back to the engine rooms. This passage was for the convenience of the force coaling the ship. At the end of the passage near the engine room was a water-tight door intended to be closed in just such a case as happened Sunday night. It is quite likely that when the collision occurred several compartments were crushed in and the water rushed down this passage before the water-tight doors could be closed. This must have flooded the engine rooms, put out the lights, and finally stopped the operation of the wireless system. It is conceivable that her injury was so great that she filled and went down by the head with just time enough to get up the women and children and get them into the lifeboats. It is remarkable that the meagre dispatches make no mention of any passengers in life preservers or of saving anyone from a life raft. It has been suspected that after lowering the boats with the women and children, the men passengers were ordered to their cabins.

Neither explanation was accurate, and no one aboard the ship knew the precise nature of the damage. Not until decades later when the wreck was discovered at a depth of about two and a half miles and was thoroughly explored did anyone find out just what the fateful blue berg did to the largest moving thing ever fashioned by man.

Captain Smith summoned Thomas Andrews, the ship's designer who was aboard as the head of a nine-member Harland and Wolff team helping Ismay decide what changes, if any, should

At the time of the sinking, it was believed that the Titanic *had collided head on with the iceberg. Had that been the case, most likely the vessel would have remained afloat and would have returned to port for repairs.*

be made in the layout of the liner. While he awaited Andrews, Boxhall reported that the mail room was flooding and that the postal clerks were busy moving their mail sacks to a higher level.

Chief Officer Henry Wilde reported to the bridge and asked if the damage was serious. After hearing Boxhall's report, the captain responded, "Certainly. It is more than serious." Turning to the ship's commutator, a device showing if a vessel was listing to one side or the other or by the bow or the stern, Smith saw that his ship was listing five degrees to starboard and two degrees down by the bow. He stared at the instrument for a short time and whispered, "Oh, my God!" so softly that only Boxhall heard him.

Ismay had been in his cabin, reviewing the plans of the *Titanic* and making notations about possible minor changes in the layout of the vessel. He put his coat on over his pajamas and put on a pair of carpet slippers before making his way to the bridge. He asked Smith, "Do you think the ship is seriously damaged?"

"I'm afraid she is," the captain answered.

As soon as Andrews arrived, he and Smith began to inspect the vessel. They found the forward cargo holds flooding, the mail room flooding, the squash courts flooding, and boiler rooms five

Because the published passenger and survivor lists were incomplete and often erroneous, a British insurance company advertised for information regarding passengers aboard the Titanic *who might have been policy holders.*

and six flooding. In the bowels of the liner, Andrews talked briefly with badly shaken stoker Fred Barrett, who was in boiler room number six well aft of watertight bulkhead number five when the collision took place. Barrett reported that he heard "a roar like thunder" when a big jet of saltwater burst into the ship. Because the watertight doors had already been closed from the bridge, he was forced to climb an emergency ladder to make his escape.

Back on the bridge Andrews noted that there was water in each of the first six watertight compartments, but the ship's designer had no way to determine its depth. He pointed out that the ship could float with any two of her watertight compartments flooded, possibly four. A design flaw became apparent to him as he saw that the first two and the last five watertight bulkheads extended only as high as D Deck, but the middle eight went only as far as E Deck. The weight of the water in the first six compartments would pull the ship down by the bow until the water in the flooded compartments rose above the top of the bulkheads. When the fifth compartment filled, it would pull down the sixth until it filled, and the sixth would pull down the seventh and so on until the ship sank. He shook his head while mumbling that she was likely to stay afloat for an hour and a half, two hours at most.

By the time Andrews had finished his summation for Smith and Ismay, Fourth Officer Boxhall had completed his rather tedious task of calculating the position of the *Titanic* without the benefit of shooting the sun. It has never been determined if his reckoning was accurate. According to him, the liner was at 41°46' north latitude and 50°14' longitude west. It was this position that Smith personally took to Phillips in the Marconi room so that the senior operator could amend the first distress signals from the liner whose call letters were MGY. At Cape Race, Newfoundland, the first message from the stricken liner had been logged at 12:10 A.M. Fifteen minutes later the Cape Race operators received the revised position information.

All accounts indicate that Smith, who had not faced disaster during his forty-three years at sea, ordered Chief Officer Wilde to uncover the lifeboats at 12:05 A.M. and sent word to the passengers that they must abandon ship about the time the first wireless call for help was dispatched. Why he waited so long to take this action is unknown since he went down with his ship.

Boxhall roused the remaining ship's officers. Murdoch oversaw the assembling of the passengers.

"What a way to begin a day," grumbled a first-class passenger as he learned that lifeboats were being lowered. "Sunday was perfect—but that was yesterday."

8

ARCHIBALD GRACIE

FATE AT WORK

COL. ARCHIBALD GRACIE, U.S. Army, retired, had never met a stranger. Within minutes of meeting someone, the old campaigner was engaged in lively conversation with his new acquaintance, and his full attention focused entirely on the other person. Gracie's gentle questions, far from brusque or probing, almost always evoked immediate responses. Much of the time, the two conversationalists quickly found a mutually interesting topic to discuss.

Aboard the *Titanic* the wealthy professional military officer was conversing with Isidor Straus before the liner left Southampton. By the evening of the first day he was acquainted with Mrs. J. J. Brown. A few days later it was Gracie who lifted the buxom woman into a lifeboat, although she was not aware of the identity of the person who saved her life.

By the second evening of the delightfully smooth and fast voyage, the resident of Washington, D.C., had gathered around him a group of especially compatible men. After listening to a concert by the ship's musicians in the Palm Room, he and his new friends—the group he called "my coterie"—invariably adjourned to the smoking room for a long conversation.

Maj. Archibald Butt, military aide to President William Howard Taft, always held the attention of his listeners when he began recounting an experience with a high-level federal official. Both John B. Thayer of the Pennsylvania Railroad and George D. Widener of Philadelphia did more listening than talking, but they enjoyed the informal sessions so much that they seldom left them early.

Artist Frank D. Millet, whose name was then well known in the United States, had many interests in addition to his vocation.

Both Arthur Ryerson and James Clinch Smith, to whom Gracie was a kindred spirit, were inclined to challenge casually some of the things the others had to say. Clarence Moore, also a resident of the nation's capital, kept the group laughing for a solid hour one evening. He once went to Kentucky with a newspaper reporter who wanted an interview with a participant in the Hatfield-McCoy feud and while there was "privileged to follow a bloodhound for nearly half a day."

Gracie always had the latest information about distances and speed. On Sunday evening, April 14, he informed them that they had traveled 546 miles that day and he had heard that the distance might be greater the next day. "If so," he announced, "we'll reach New York early and perhaps set a speed record for a crossing in this season."

Charles H. Hays, president of Canada's Grand Trunk Railroad, usually listened without making more than perfunctory remarks. His facial expression clearly revealed that he was surprised by Gracie's report. Speaking slowly and emphatically, he revealed his personal views—about which he had earlier said nothing—concerning the lucrative North Atlantic trade.

"The White Star, the Cunard, and the Hamburg-American Lines are devoting their attention and ingenuity to vie with one another to attain supremacy in luxurious ships and in making speed records. The time will come," he warned, "when this will lead to a disaster of some sort. I'm sorry to say so, but I regard such an outcome as inevitable."

As the discussion meandered to a close, Gracie looked up and saw Isidor Straus approaching with a book in his hand. He rose to greet the department store executive, who returned the copy of *The Truth about Chickamauga* and thanked him for his kindness in lending it. Earlier, Gracie had confided to him that his cousin, Theodore Roosevelt, had encouraged him to write a new account of one of the most celebrated battles of the Civil War. The undertaking had required an immense amount of time and energy, and Gracie made no secret of his pride in his work when it was published in Boston in 1911.

A gentleman of the old school and inherently polite, Straus had told the military officer a bit about his personal experiences in the Civil War that had cost the life of the first Archibald Gracie. "Now I know why that battle is often called 'bloody Chickamauga,' " he said. "You have made a splendid case for the fact that

Col. Archibald Gracie had retired from the U.S. army and found his fortune in real estate. As a man of leisure he had become an amateur historian. Just prior to his voyage abroad Gracie had written a study of the battle of Chickamauga during the Civil War, mostly as a means of exculpating the reputation of his grandfather, Archibald Gracie Jr.

though his losses were very high, the grandfather whose name you bear did the best he could with what he had."

West Point graduate Gracie appreciated that verdict. Many accounts of the battle had castigated Confederate Brig. Gen. Archibald Gracie for what some called "inept leadership" during the two-hour period in which nearly one thousand men under his command were killed or wounded. As he approached retirement, his grandson from Alabama set out to write a book that would show precisely why the general could have done nothing else at Chickamauga. When he launched the project, Colonel Gracie had had no idea that it would dominate his life for seven years.

Since the smoking room coterie broke up when Straus arrived, Gracie went to his stateroom and promptly fell asleep. Looking back upon that never-to-be-forgotten evening, he wrote, "I cannot regard it as a mere coincidence that on this particular Sunday night I was thus prompted to retire early for nearly three hours of invigorating sleep, whereas an accident occurring at midnight of any of the four preceding days would have found me mentally and physically tired."

Awakened after midnight by what appeared to be a slight jarring of the smooth passage of the *Titanic* through increasingly cold waters, Gracie's first thought was of the gravity with which Charles Hays had spoken of an impending disaster. He pulled on a loose

Gracie enjoyed the unbreachable male bastion of the first-class smoking room (above) on the Promenade Deck. The mahogany-paneled walls were inset with leaded glass and etched-patterned mirrors, and the room was decorated with leather-covered armchairs and carved, marble-topped tables.

garment, went on deck, and found men and women milling about without having taken time to dress properly. "There was not the slightest indication of panic," he later wrote. "Some fragments of ice had fallen on the deck and these were picked up and passed around by some of the facetious ones, who offered them as mementoes of the occasion." Like other veteran world travelers, Gracie was aware that icebergs frequently dotted the North Atlantic during late winter and early spring; hence he did not take the frozen debris lightly.

By the time he returned to his compartment, donned warm clothing, and came back on deck, dozens of puzzled persons were congregated there. Few if any of them were frightened; they took seriously the publicity that the *Titanic* was invulnerable. Still, they did not know what had happened, and a few wondered if there was trouble in the engine room. "Is it possible," someone asked, "that we've burned up all the coal taken aboard at Southampton?"

Unlike most passengers in first class, Gracie had gone out of his way to become acquainted with the ship's officers—including Captain Smith, who had provided him with daily reports of the distance traveled the previous day. Ascending to the boat deck, he found Second Officer Charles H. Lightoller supervising the loading of a lifeboat. At Lightoller's nod, he began assisting ladies and an occasional child.

One of the people he remembered most vividly was Mrs. John Jacob Astor—known to her friends, Gracie included, as Madeline. Since she was visibly pregnant, he was careful to lift her gently into lifeboat number four. Her husband of a few months was standing as close to her as possible. The great-grandson of America's first millionaire asked if he could accompany his wife. "No, sir," Lightoller replied. "No men are allowed in these boats until women are loaded first." At that, the wealthiest man in the United States asked what boat this was so that he would be able to find his wife later, and Gracie turned his attention to other ladies. One of them, Miss Edith Evans, stubbornly resisted efforts to get her into a boat. After a brief struggle, Gracie gave up. He recalled her telling him that in London she had experienced a premonition of "meeting death on water," and so he assumed she did not wish to be saved.

As lifeboat number two was being loaded, a few men pushed their way into it, Gracie later said. Lightoller handed his volunteer assistant his pistol, told him to order the men out of the boat, and to fire the weapon to emphasize that he meant it. About that time J. Clinch Smith ran along the now-slanting deck, shouting repeatedly, "Any more ladies?"

All of the standard lifeboats having been lowered, members of the crew turned their attention to special boats designed by a Danish engineer and named for him. Englehardt boats were often termed "collapsible," but in his written account of the tragedy, Gracie emphasized that this was misleading. They did have canvas along their edges, he noted, but except for their relatively small size they were in other respects much like the sixteen huge lifeboats that regulations required the *Titanic* to carry.

Since all four of these were on top of the boat deck, it was especially difficult to get them into a position where they could be used.

*Naturally, the White Star Line
provided matches for its passengers
throughout the ship.*

Gracie helped with these boats. As the last of them was dropped into the sea, he tried an expedient that he had learned while surfing, and he "rode a wave" to the top of the officers' quarters. After briefly clinging to his precarious position, he decided he'd be better off in the water, and so he tried to jump from the *Titanic*. Since he was loaded down with "a heavy long-skirted overcoat with Norfolk coat beneath and a clumsy life-preserver over all," his attempt to leap into the water failed.

Still on the roof and panting from his fruitless exertion, Gracie felt the mighty liner lunge downward, creating a huge upward wave by its dive. This surge washed Gracie into the open sea—no longer sixty feet below the boat deck. Recalling a few dramatic instants, he wrote: "Down, down, I went: it seemed a great distance. There was a very noticeable pressure upon my ears. . . . When under water I retained, as it appears, a sense of general direction, and, as soon as I could do so, swam away from the starboard side of the ship, as I knew my life depended upon it. I swam with all my strength, and I seemed endowed with an extra supply for the occasion. I was incited to desperate effort by the thought of boiling water, or steam, from the expected explosion of the ship's boilers, and that I would be scalded to death." The retired officer said that even while struggling to save his life, he was conscious that "the plunge in the icy water produced no sense of coldness whatever, and I had no thought of cold until later on."

Gracie found "a piece of wreckage like a wooden crate," so he clung to it with all of his strength. "There was no one alive or struggling in the water or calling for aid in the immediate vicinity of where I arose to the surface," he recalled. "I threw my right leg over the wooden crate in an attempt to straddle and balance myself on top of it, but I turned over in a somersault with it under water."

When he rose to the surface again, his ears and his brain were assaulted as they had never been before: "There arose to the sky the most horrible sounds ever heard by mortal man except those of us who survived this terrible tragedy. The agonizing cries of death from over a thousand throats, the wails and groans of the suffering, the shrieks of the terror-stricken and the awful gaspings for breath of those in the last throes of drowning, none of us will ever forget to our dying day."

A considerable distance to his left, Gracie spotted one of the Englehardt boats overturned in the water. On top of it a dozen or so men, judged by their dress to be members of the crew, were precariously perched. After what he termed "a considerable swim," the colonel reached the boat and expected to be extended half a dozen helping hands. None came, he said, so he grabbed the arm of a young sailor and managed to throw his right leg upon the boat. Someone whose name he never learned then helped him get into a reclining position. Afterward "came a dozen other swimmers who clambered around and whom we helped aboard."

Reflecting upon that dreadful night, Gracie remembered: "I had no time to contemplate danger when there was continuous need of quick thought, action and composure withal. Had I become rattled for a moment, or in the slightest degree been undecided during the several emergencies cited, I am certain that I never should have lived to tell the tale of my miraculous escape."

A few hours later, as Gracie, bruised and weary, climbed the rope ladder that swung from the deck of the *Carpathia,* the retired officer experienced an overwhelming sense of wonder that he had managed to survive. Not until the following day did he learn that he was the last man to leave the ship and survive.

Within days after reaching New York, Gracie began work upon another book, determined to finish it quickly. Influenced perhaps by the title of his earlier publication on the battle of Chickamauga, he produced the manuscript of *The Truth About the Titanic* in less than six months, but he did not live to see it published in 1913. His death, his relatives and friends agreed, was the result of the extreme physical and mental ordeal to which he was subjected in the early morning hours of April 15, 1912. Incredibly, the last person to get off the *Titanic* and reach the haven of the Cunard rescue ship was the first of more than seven hundred survivors to die.

9

ARCHIBALD BUTT AND FRANK MILLET

DAMON AND PYTHIAS

MAJ. ARCHIBALD BUTT looked up from his desk at the figure standing in the doorway of his White House office. "How in the world did you get in here?"

Frank Davis Millet smiled broadly. "I don't need a pass; I'm here so often everybody thinks I'm a member of the staff," he responded. "But seriously, I'm here because we had a talk about you at the club last night. All of the fellows agree with me. You need to have some time off, and I decided you should go to Rome with me."

Butt shook his head but said nothing. He was caught between the two men he admired most—Theodore Roosevelt and William Howard Taft—as they vied for their party's presidential nomination in 1912. Butt had served both in the White House as military aide, close friend, and confidant, but now both were feuding and both wanted his loyalty. Unable to choose between them, Butt had fallen into depression and finally requested reassignment.

Seeing the physical marks of the strain on his friend, Millet continued, hoping to convince his friend to get away from the political brouhaha. "You've been lots of places, I know. But Rome is in a class by itself. If you won't speak to the president about a little vacation, I'm going to do it, myself."

That evening, Richard B. Watrous, secretary of the American Civic Association, joined Millet and Butt at the capital city's Metropolitan Club. He later told a reporter for the *New York Times* that "he witnessed the manner in which Millet pleaded with Major Butt to go to Europe with him for a rest."

When President Taft's military aide refused to ask for time off, the renowned artist went to the chief executive and told him that

Butt's noticeable pallor was a source of concern. As secretary of the president's Commission on Fine Arts, Millet had access to the chief executive and was frequently seen with him. Taft initially hesitated to dispense with Butt's services for even a few weeks but gave his hearty consent when Millet pulled the clincher of his argument. "We can time my business in Rome so that we will come back on the *Titanic*," he pointed out.

Mutual friends of the pair knew that Butt was a bachelor who lived in an elegant old mansion and that Millet's wife was living at his family home in Cotswolds, England. Time after time, a club member who saw them approaching together called out, "Here come Damon and Pythias again!" in reference to the Greek legend of the two loyal friends.

Millet was responsible for acquiring new quarters for the American Academy of Fine Arts in Rome and spent six weeks in the winter of 1911–12 inspecting possible sites. He made key selections and returned to Washington just as Taft came home from a strenuous campaign tour. Although he publicly emphasized that he depended heavily upon Butt, Taft's own weariness may have entered into his approval of Millet's idea.

Once the Millet-Butt trip was in the planning stage, the chief executive decided that since his aide often served as a courier, it would be convenient to have him deliver a personal message to Pope Pius X. He could look after this and other official matters while Millet was busy closing the purchase of property.

MILLET WAS among the most distinguished artists of the period, and he executed several historical works such as "Wandering Thoughts," "At the Inn," and "Between Two Fires." His works were collected on both sides of the Atlantic, but while his art was popular, very few photographs were ever taken of him. Born in Massachusetts in 1846, he presented himself to a recruiting officer in the third year of the Civil War. Although the officer was desperately eager to fill his quota, a single glance told him that Millet's age could not be overlooked. So he pointed toward a band of musicians and told the fifteen-year-old that he could not join the army, but he might be permitted to join the regimental band. As a result, young Millet went to war as a drummer boy in the Sixtieth Massachusetts Regiment.

During the war, a surgeon lost one of his assistants in battle, and so he requisitioned Millet as a substitute aide. Upon being discharged at the war's conclusion, Millet won admission to Harvard College and then pursued a career in journalism after graduation. Working first for the *Boston Advertiser* and then the *Boston Courier,* he gained experience that led publishers to name him editor of the *Boston Sunday Evening Gazette.*

Having always been deeply interested in art, at the age of twenty-six Millet gave up his job and used his savings to spend a year at the Royal Academy in Antwerp, Belgium. His spectacular success at the academy and his residence in Europe made him a natural choice as an American representative at an exposition held in Vienna. There he became acquainted with Charles Francis Adams and formed a lasting friendship with the man who served as the American ambassador to Great Britain.

Millet covered the Vienna exposition for two New York newspapers, and when the event closed he returned home and was soon given a position with the Philadelphia exposition that was held in the country's centennial year of 1876. Afterward Millet took on the task of war correspondent for the *New York Herald* and soon was on a battlefield covering the struggle between Russia and Turkey. There "whistling bullets gave vividness to his pencil, and hard rides to post dispatches taught him the country." Millet was assigned to a Russian camp and added vivid sketches to his war news dispatches to the *Herald.* Simultaneously, he was recognized as both a correspondent and an artist. Few Americans have received the numerous honors conferred upon him. In the name of the czar, Millet was awarded the Cross of Saint Stanislaus and the Cross of Saint Anne. In addition to these decorations, after accompanying Russian troops to Constantinople, he was decorated with the Iron Cross of Rumania.

Now so well known that he could pick almost any journalistic post he wanted, at war's end Millet joined the staff of the *London Daily News* and later went to the *London Graphic* as an artist. He left the largest city in the world to become a director of the 1893 World's Columbian Exposition—an event at which the Americans were determined to eclipse the earlier international events held in Vienna, Paris, and London.

When war broke out between Spain and the United States, Millet was eager to be with the first troops to face Spanish bullets. His dispatches about the Spanish-American War ran in the *London Times* as well as the *New York Sun* and *Harper's Weekly.* Subsequently made a chevalier of the French Legion of Honor and

THE MARINERS' MUSEUM

Maj. Archibald Butt was a military aide to President William Howard Taft just as he had been to the previous occupant of the White House, Theodore Roosevelt. The feud that had broken out between Taft and Roosevelt had caught Butt in the crossfire, and he had taken six weeks' vacation in Italy to recuperate from depression.

decorated with Japan's First Class Order of the Sacred Treasure, he was among the most decorated of Americans when he left his wife in England and settled in Washington as President Taft's chief adviser concerning the arts.

Millet honestly did not want to become director of the American Academy of Arts in Rome, but the institution was faced with a financial crisis and that influenced him to take the post. Once he had traveled to Rome, he became entranced with the beauty of the time-hallowed city. If he could be so easily enraptured, he believed that his friend, Butt, might find a respite in Rome from the political bickering that had so depressed him lately.

ARCHIBALD BUTT was born in Augusta, Georgia, and for a number of years served as the Washington correspondent for several newspapers. His stories and byline regularly appeared in the *Louisville Post,* the *Atlanta Constitution,* the *Nashville Banner,* the *Augusta Chronicle,* and the *Savannah Morning News.*

Butt spent a period in Mexico as secretary to the legation, then returned to Washington and began to write novels after resuming his role as newspaper correspondent. Maj. Gen. H. C. Corbin, who served as adjutant general of the U.S. Army during the Spanish-American War, promoted Butt to captain and dispatched him to the Philippines to take command of a regiment of volunteers.

Captain Butt departed from San Francisco with a cargo of five hundred mules destined for Honolulu. Although he had been instructed to unload the animals when the island was reached, Butt refused to leave them where forage and stable costs were so high he feared they would be abused. Not a mule died during the long voyage to the Philippines, and while stationed there the captain wrote several articles about the handling of animals in the tropics. One of them caught the eye of Theodore Roosevelt, who soon "had him detailed to duty as one of his personal aides."

The newspaper noted that Butt "kept up with Roosevelt in all his physical stunts, climbed the heights of Rock Creek Canyon with the President, and reduced the handling of crowds at the White House receptions to a fine art. He made the record there of remembering the names and introducing 1,280 persons in one hour. Major Butt was an ideal clubman, for he knew everyone and was liked by all."

Since both Butt and Millet had extensive experience as newspaper correspondents and both had taken part in the

Spanish-American War, it was natural that they should be drawn together as soon as they became acquainted.

As SOON as the garbled news about the sinking of the *Titanic* began trickling into wireless rooms around the world, President Taft began bombarding shipping officials and the media with questions about his aide. Beginning on April 16, the *New York Times* published brief stories concerning the president's anxiety about Butt. Described as "stunned" after hearing at the theater that the great liner might be lost, Taft was joyful when afternoon papers reported that all of the passengers had been saved.

"He was nearly frantic when he learned the truth about 11:00 on April 17, and went at once to the telegraph room at the White House to read bulletins," according to the *Times*. Telegraph operators of the War and Navy Departments were notified that they must immediately send to the president "anything they might get from the wireless stations." Readers of the newspaper were told that Butt's "fidelity, practical sense, and jovial nature made him exactly the sort of a comrade that a man worried with innumerable heavy burdens would desire to have near him."

At the Brooklyn Navy Yard, the Marconi operator caught a message from the *Salem* to the *Carpathia:* "The President of the United States is very anxious to know if Major Butt, Mr. Millet, and Mr. Moore [of Washington] are safe. Please inform me at once so that I can transmit to him."

When the truth about the *Titanic* became apparent, Taft was described as "turning like a man who has been stunned by a heavy blow." Certain that the liner had been lost, but unwilling to accept the fact that Butt was not saved, he inundated White Star Line Vice President P. A. S. Franklin with telegrams asking for "the very latest news about survivors." Taft's brother made a personal visit to Franklin's office but learned only that the names of Butt, Millet, and tennis star Karl H. Behr were not on the list of those who had reached the *Carpathia*.

A brief notice in the *Times* of April 18 appeared with a Washington dateline of April 17. Headlines informed the public that TAFT STILL HOPES FOR BUTT—REFUSES TO BELIEVE ALL CHANCE OF AIDE'S RESCUE IS GONE. Since wireless messages from the *Carpathia* were chiefly personal notes sent by those aboard, the president was quoted as saying that he believed "something definite might be known" when the rescue ship docked.

Butt (above right) could not choose between Taft (above left) and Roosevelt and tried to maintain his close friendship with both.

In Paris and Rome, the people talked of nothing but the disaster in the North Atlantic. The pope and Cardinal Merry del Val were so concerned over the fate of Butt that they sent a cablegram to the apostolic delegation in Washington asking for news of him. King Victor Emanuel III of Italy expressed his condolences. French states-man Clément-Armand Fallières cabled Taft his regrets, sharing Taft's "anguish about the fate of your aid and friend, Major Butt."

At the *Times,* editors were more realistic than Taft. When most of a page was devoted to an early list of survivors on April 18, the news-paper carried a lengthy story that was largely an obituary for Butt.

Still unwilling to give up on Butt, Taft ordered the scout cruis-ers *Salem* and *Chester* to proceed at full steam to the scene of the *Titanic*'s sinking to search for other survivors. By the time she was forty miles off the Chesapeake Cape, the *Chester* was making twenty knots an hour. Despite this fast progress, the newspapers noted "there seems no hope at all that they will find survivors."

There were no additional survivors. Only those passengers and crewmen from the *Titanic* who managed to reach the *Carpathia*

So anxious was Taft for news of Butt's fate when he heard of the sinking of the Titanic *that he even sent his brother to the White Star Line office in New York for the latest word.*

TAFT'S BROTHER IN WHITE STAR CROWD

Sought News of Major Butt, of Whom No Word Has Been Obtainable.

WATCHERS ARE LOSING HOPE

Wireless from Scout Cruiser Said Names of All Cabin Passengers Saved Had Been Sent In.

were saved; four of those taken aboard the lone rescue ship were dead on arrival.

THE DETAILS concerning the last hours of the man who served as an aide to two presidents and his artist friend are meager and contradictory. On Sunday evening, Butt attended the Widener reception for Captain Smith and then went to the smoking room. Hours later, when the loading of the lifeboats was well under way, Col. Archibald Gracie caught a brief glimpse of a group of men sitting around a table in the first-class smoking room. A man whom he failed to see clearly was with Butt, Millet, and Clarence Moore—the man was later identified as Arthur Ryerson, a steel magnate—and the four were playing bridge. "All four seemed oblivious of what was going on on the decks outside," Gracie reported. "It is impossible to suppose that they did not know of the collision with an iceberg and that the room they were in had been deserted by all others. It occurred to me that these men desired to show their entire indifference to the danger."

Gracie never saw Butt and Millet again, but another survivor, Marie Young, who had been music governess for Theodore Roosevelt's children, described Major Butt's escorting her to lifeboat number eight, and recalled that he "wrapped blankets about me and tucked me in as carefully as if we were going on a motor ride." Then he stepped back, lifted his hat to her, and said, "Goodbye, Miss Young. Good luck to you, and don't forget to remember me to the folks back home."

Another survivor told a *Times* reporter that she noticed Butt on the bridge five minutes before the last lifeboat was lowered.

When informed of her account, Gracie repeated that he was sure both Butt and Millet had remained on A Deck and went down with the ship. A surviving room steward whose name was not noted testified before a committee of the U.S. Senate that he "saw Butt and Benjamin Guggenheim on the upper deck, talking calmly with Mr. Astor." Another survivor, Dr. Washington Dodge, recalled that Butt and Astor had gone down together: "They went down standing on the bridge, side by side. I could not mistake them."

Mrs. Henry B. Harris was quoted in newspapers as having written a graphic eulogy about the officer, age forty-one, who had been on intimate terms with two presidents. According to a 1912 volume by Logan Marshall, she said:

> The world should rise in praise of Major Butt. That man's conduct will remain in my memory forever. The American army is honored by him and the way he taught some of the other men how to behave when women and children were suffering that awful mental fear of death. Major Butt was near me [at a time not stated] and I noticed everything that he did.
>
> He helped the sailors rearrange the rope or chain that had gone wrong and lifted some of the women in with a touch of gallantry. Not only was there a complete lack of any fear in his manner, but there was the action of an aristocrat.
>
> When the time came he was a man to be feared. In one of the earlier boats fifty women, it seemed, were about to be lowered, when a man, suddenly panic-stricken, ran to the stern of it. Major Butt shot one arm out, caught him by the back of the neck and jerked him backward like a pillow. His head cracked against a rail and he was stunned.
>
> "Sorry," said Major Butt, "women will be attended to first or I'll break every damned bone in your body."

Marshall discovered evidence that caused him to describe Butt's last hours in a different fashion: "A number of steerage passengers were yelling and screaming and fighting to get to the boats. Officers drew guns and told them that if they moved towards the boat they would be shot dead. Major Butt had a gun in his hand and covered the men who tried to get to the boats."

Similarly, a widely circulated tale that Millet was among steerage passengers urging the women and children into the lifeboats is debatable. Still another tale that surfaced as soon as the *Carpathia*

Frank Millet had the heart of an adventurer as much as his friend Butt. In 1861, at the age of fifteen, he tried to enlist in the Union army, but being underage he was allowed to join the regimental band as a drummer boy, much like the young patriot pictured here.

reached New York was carried in the *Times* and stated that Butt reputedly agreed to shoot George D. Widener, John Jacob Astor, and Isidor Straus first and then shoot himself before the boat sank. "It is said that this agreement had been carried out," readers of the *Times* were informed.

Of these conflicting accounts, Gracie's guess that Damon and Pythias showed their courage by remaining on A Deck and going down with the ship is the most plausible. Regardless of how they spent their last hour, the deaths of the two men who had little of the wealth for which numerous other passengers were noted were grouped with them by members of the general public. Elbert Hubbard, famous for his book *A Message to Garcia*, summed up what thousands thought but were not quite able to express.

The names of the dead men with whom Hubbard was personally acquainted were ticked off one by one: Straus, Stead, Astor, Butt, Harris, Thayer, Widener, Guggenheim, and Hays. Writing that he thought he knew them earlier, Hubbard confessed that he did not guess their greatness then. "These dead have not lived and died in vain," he wrote. "They have brought us all a little nearer together—we think better of our kind."

10

JOHN JACOB ASTOR

JJA OR AV?

TRAVELING FIRST class, naturally, were John Jacob Astor IV and his pregnant wife, Madeline, who boarded the *Titanic* at Cherbourg, France. Astor would have preferred to remain anonymous, but that was impossible. He did little more than exchange casual comments with those who sat with him at the dining table or near him during concerts in the Palm Room. Hence no one remembered anything of consequence about his shipboard activities before late Sunday evening when it was reluctantly accepted that "it looks like some of us may be in for a bad time."

Since there was no public address system on the ship, Captain Smith's order that passengers don life jackets had to be delivered room to room by the ship's stewards. This ominous directive prompted scores of first-class passengers to congregate on the decks and wonder what was going on, showing few signs of apprehension. Some knew that there had been an impact; a small number had found ice on the deck and were aware that the ship had collided with an iceberg. Even after obeying the captain's order and preparing for survival in the water, most men and women who chatted on the decks expected the evening to be little more than "a training exercise by which it would be vividly demonstrated that an ocean liner can be evacuated quickly and efficiently."

Astor had heard about the iceberg and gone up to the boat deck to see what was happening. At the time, the situation was still being investigated by the crew, and so he returned to his cabin and explained to his wife that the ship had struck a berg but the matter did not seem serious. When the couple were later notified by a steward to dress and go on deck with their life jackets, they responded casually, and Mrs. Astor took her time dressing. When she did emerge from their room, she looked as if she were prepared for a shopping excursion. She wore a black broadtail coat with a sable collar and a diamond necklace and carried a muff.

Around 1:15 Monday morning, Astor and his wife were in the gymnasium, according to several survivors' accounts. One such observer was Bride, the Marconi operator, who recalled seeing Astor take a penknife and casually open a life jacket to show his wife the cork that made it float. Bride might have protested such destruction of ship's property under ordinary circumstances, but he was intimately aware of the ship's dire state. Consequently, he hurried back to his post.

On deck somewhat later, Archibald Gracie spotted a bright light, apparently not far away. He pointed it out "to reassure a group of ladies" of whom he had taken special charge. Overhearing this, Astor asked Gracie to point out the light for him. Both men leaned over the rail of the ship and looked "close in towards the bow" but had to move out of the way quickly to avoid being hit by a lifeboat being "made ready with its gunwale lowered to the level of the floor of the Boat Deck above us and obstructing our view."

To Gracie and Astor's disappointment the light that they thought should be growing brighter became increasingly dim and then vanished altogether. Others had also seen the light and took courage from it, which gave rise to tales about a mystery ship being close to the *Titanic* that for reasons unknown ignored the hobbled ocean liner's rockets and other distress signals.

Just before 2:00 A.M., Second Officer Lightoller turned his attention to the last conventional lifeboat on the liner. About an hour earlier he had started to prepare it for a line of women who had queued in anticipation of its use. Lightoller, however, was called to another boat, and most of the women waited more or less patiently for his return.

Survivors later listed for *New York Times* reporters some of those who stood in this line. Mrs. George D. Widener of Philadelphia— Eleanor to her friends—was joined by Mrs. Arthur Ryerson, and the two talked of an upcoming charity ball as they waited. Mrs. John B. Thayer and Mrs. William Carter stepped back to make room for unidentified maids and children, two survivors remembered. "Young Mrs. Astor," as she was commonly called, fidgeted

DICTIONARY OF AMERICAN PORTRAITS

John Jacob Astor IV was returning to the United States after spending time in England, Egypt, and Paris with his second wife, Madeline, who was four months pregnant.

nervously. "Poor thing, she must have been dreadfully uncomfortable and might have feared that the commotion would bring on labor," Mrs. J. J. "Maggie" Brown was quoted as having remarked.

Astor stood as close to his wife as he could without joining the queue of ladies, and his face brightened when he saw lifeboat number four finally descending toward the waiting passengers. Of all the ship's lifeboats, this would be the most difficult to load. The ladies had to negotiate a stack of deck chairs arranged as stairs and be passed through *Titanic*'s windows into the boat. By this time the ship was listing so sharply that Lightoller had to use a cable and hook to pull in the boat so the women could climb into it. Standing with one foot on deck and the other in the boat, he tried to assist each person aboard. Astor saw the awkward position of the officer and stepped forward to help.

Madeline Astor yielded her place in line and hung back. Finally, her husband said, "Get into the lifeboat, to please me." She was the last person to enter the lifeboat just as Lightoller began shouting instructions to lower it to the sea. Astor asked the officer if he could join his wife, explaining that she was pregnant. Half a dozen survivors said that they heard him do so. Physically and mentally exhausted, Lightoller gave the world's wealthiest man a gentle no, adding that "no men are allowed in these boats until the women are loaded first."

Astor asked what boat this was and then turned to his wife and said, "The sea is calm. You'll be all right. You're in good hands. I'll meet you in the morning." He quietly stepped back, and the lifeboat, carrying about thirty people, soon disappeared from his sight. Many believe that Astor then went below to release his Airedale from its cage on F Deck. Days later Madeline allegedly claimed that she had spotted their dog, Kitty, dashing along the ship's sloping deck as the lifeboat pulled away. Those dubious of her claim commented, "Her eyesight must have been truly remarkable."

Gracie claimed that it was he who lifted Madeline Astor "over the four-foot high rail of the ship through the frame." Her husband, he added, "held her left arm as we carefully passed her to Lightoller, who seated her in the boat." Astor may not have known that the lifeboat was designed to carry sixty-five people and was considerably less than half full when it started its twenty-five-foot descent to the sea. Gracie was acutely aware of this but was helpless to do anything about it.

Testifying before a committee of the U.S. Senate a few days after reaching New York aboard the rescue ship *Carpathia,* Lightoller said he put thirty passengers in lifeboat number four "with two seamen to row." If his count was accurate, there was enough room for at least thirty-three more people in one of the last lifeboats to leave the stricken ship.

Responding to questions from a *Times* reporter, Gracie was emphatic in praising Astor: "The conduct of Colonel John Jacob Astor was deserving of the highest praise. This wealthy New Yorker devoted all his energy to saving his young bride." When the lifeboat he had tried to enter departed without him, "Colonel Astor then inquired the number of the boat, and turned to the work of clearing the other boats and in reassuring the frightened and nervous women."

In his published account, Gracie mentioned Astor's inquiry about the number of the lifeboat in which his wife sat, but he contradicted his earlier statement about what took place when lifeboat number four left. "Colonel Astor," he wrote, "moved away from this point and I never saw him again."

In New York the news that Astor went down with the ship was met with incredulity. The editors of the *New York American,* who mistakenly believed the death toll exceeded eighteen hundred, devoted many columns to Astor and virtually ignored the others who perished with him. On April 18 the *Times* informed its readers that Vincent Astor would meet the *Carpathia* on his father's steam yacht, the *Noma,* to bring his stepmother to shore.

Vincent's grief was characterized as pitiable. When his father's name did not appear on the first "slender list that had been wirelessed from the *Carpathia*," he stayed up all night "hoping against hope for some reassuring word." Young Astor went to the offices of the Associated Press and the Marconi Company and reputedly stood for a long time reading bulletins posted by the *Times* on its huge outdoor billboard.

Described as having been "a delicate child," Vincent was born in the family mansion at the site where the Waldorf-Astoria Hotel was later built. During most of his early years, he spent about half of his time at his father's country home on the Hudson River. When his mother, Ava Willing Astor, secured a divorce in 1909, her former husband was given custody of their son. In 1910 he was with his father aboard the yacht *Nourmahal* when it was briefly believed to have been lost in the West Indies.

Since the first Mrs. Astor had entered into a prenuptial agreement, she was not eligible to receive the then-standard "widow's third of the estate," but would presumably continue for a time to receive alimony of fifty thousand dollars annually. Not quite twenty-one years old, Vincent was the chief beneficiary of his father, who left behind a fortune estimated at between $100 million and $200 million.

THE MAN who went down on the *Titanic* had inherited what was generally believed to be the largest fortune in America. His great-grandfather, German-born John Jacob Astor, had immigrated to America in 1786 and en route to the New World had heard that a great deal of money could be made in the fur trade. He moved into the business in a small way but eventually won a virtual monopoly for his American Fur Company, then he took his immense profits and invested in Manhattan farmland. His estate was estimated at more than $20 million, which his son, William Backhouse Astor, inherited and doubled. William's two sons, John Jacob and William, founded the two principal branches of the family, with the elder John continuing to develop the family fortune in America and the younger William cultivating overseas in Britain.

By the beginning of the twentieth century, the American Astors owned some of the most exclusive real estate in the country as well

Astor's status as one of the wealthiest men in the world placed him atop this list of headlines in the New York Times *when the news broke that the* Titanic *had been lost.*

Col. Astor Went Down Waving Farewells to His Bride.

SOME STORIES OF PANIC

Others Say Order Was Maintained—Mrs. Straus Clung to Husband's Side.

SHOCK CALLED "SLIGHT JAR"

Card Playing Continued In the Cabin and None Realized the End Was Near.

as some of the most deplorable. While they were hardly embarrassed to be slumlords, the Astors were also philanthropic. William Backhouse bequeathed four hundred thousand dollars to New York City to be consolidated with other donations to fund the New York Public Library.

John Jacob IV showed considerable interest in developing the family's holdings by building several hotels: the Knickerbocker, the St. Regis, and the second segment of the Waldorf-Astoria. In private he was an eccentric, a tinkerer, and an inventor with a fascination for turbine engines. He patented a bicycle brake, a storage battery, and a road construction machine. The latter, a pneumatic contrivance "for the renovation of macadam [or asphalt] roads," attracted considerable attention at the 1893 Columbian Exposition in Chicago and took a first prize. Astor also invented a steamship chair that was held in place by suction cups and "a vibratory disintegrator for getting power gas from peat." All of these inventions he "dedicated to the public" for general use without charge. He also wrote a science fiction novel, *A Journey in Other Worlds,* whose main character had been contracted by the Terrestrial Axis Straightening Company to adjust Earth's axis so the people would enjoy perpetual springtime.

As a businessman Astor had an ambitious and a ruthless side, always finding a way to get what he wanted. He was also vain. During the Spanish-American War he had raised a regiment of volunteers. Naturally, he was made colonel of the regiment. Although the unit saw almost no action during the war, Astor preferred to be addressed as colonel and wore his uniform to all official functions. The Newport mansion had an eighteen-car garage. He once commented, "A man who has a million dollars is almost as well off as if he were wealthy."

Astor lost a great deal of social standing when he divorced his wife of eighteen years in 1909 to marry eighteen-year-old Madeline Force. The scandal was not so much that he planned to marry Madeline, but rather that society would have been kinder to him had he not divorced his first wife and simply kept Madeline as his mistress. The stigma led Astor to go abroad with Madeline. They did not marry until 1911, and even then had difficulty finding a clergyman willing to perform the wedding.

SOCIAL STANDING and wealth meant nothing to the *Titanic*'s second officer as he superintended the loading and launching of lifeboats; he didn't know who Astor was at the time he denied him a place in a half-filled boat. Astor's wealth and prominence meant even less to the cold North Atlantic.

As soon as the news of the lost ship reached the White Star Line offices in North America, the company's Halifax agent, A. G. Jones and Company, chartered the *Mackay-Bennett,* a British cable-laying vessel, to recover as many victims of the sinking as possible. The vessel was loaded with tons of ice, one hundred coffins, and embalming supplies. Capt. F. H. Lardner headed an all-volunteer crew augmented by forty members of the Funeral Directors Association of the Maritime Provinces.

The *Mackay-Bennett* sailed on April 17 and reached its destination on the evening of April 20. Their work began the next morning. The sea was heavy and the wind was cold as boat after boat ventured out to collect the human debris still scattered on the surface. Fifty-one bodies were recovered the first day. Each

*The Astor family had extensive real estate holdings in
Manhattan and developed these by building several hotels.
The original Waldorf was built in 1893 on Fifth Avenue.
John Jacob Astor IV oversaw the construction of the
Astoria hotel in 1897, which was joined to the Waldorf, and
the hotel thereafter was known as The Waldorf-Astoria.*

body was numbered with a piece of canvas, and all valuables and
personal items were inventoried and placed in a small canvas bag
numbered to match the body. Complete descriptions were also
recorded for each corpse, noting its height, weight, hair and eye
color, birthmarks, scars, or tattoos.

Exposure had not been kind to the victims. Several were so
badly disfigured by a week's immersion in the sea that the
embalmers considered it pointless to carry them back to Halifax.

That evening a burial service was conducted and thirty passengers from the *Titanic* were committed to the deep.

By the end of the second day the *Mackay-Bennett* had recovered 187 bodies, and Lardner radioed Halifax that he would need assistance. Jones and Company had anticipated this and chartered a second cable vessel, the *Minia,* and she arrived on the scene on April 26. The *Mackay-Bennett* returned immediately to Halifax with 190 bodies; the *Minia* continued to search the area until May 3. When the recovery mission was over, the two ships had recovered 323 bodies; 119 were buried at sea.

When the bodies were brought ashore, careful efforts were made to preserve class distinctions. Crew members were packed in ice. Second- and third-class passengers were sewn in canvas. First-class travelers were embalmed and placed in coffins. A temporary morgue was set up in Halifax, and only next of kin or those with authorization from next of kin were allowed to enter. An office was created to issue death certificates, each of which listed the cause of death as "accidental drowning, S.S. *Titanic,* at sea."

The first body to be claimed was that of Astor by his son. It was crushed and covered with soot, leading many to conclude that Astor had been caught beneath the forward funnel when it fell into the sea. He was wearing a blue serge suit, a blue handkerchief, a gold-buckled belt, brown boots with red rubber soles, and a brown flannel shirt with his initials on the collar. The shirt was key to Vincent's identifying his father's body rather than the amount of money found on him: £225 in notes, $2,440 in American currency, £5 in gold, 7s in silver, and 50 francs.

Strangely, the blue handkerchief was marked with the initials AV. Some who have studied the lore of the sinking of the ship have speculated that Astor may have been murdered while the *Titanic* was sinking, and the killer put on his shirt but forgot to take his own handkerchief from his pocket. This piece of guesswork ignored the fact that the only AV on the ill-fated liner's passenger list was a woman and an immigrant, Adele Jane Vogel.

No one knows exactly how Astor met his fate. Lightoller had turned him away from the lifeboat in which Madeline Astor survived. Allegedly Astor saw a young boy also turned away from the lifeboat and then saved the life of ten-year-old William Carter when he placed a girl's large hat on the boy's head, turned to Lightoller, and said, "Now he's a girl, and he can go." As noted in an earlier chapter, Dr. Washington Dodge claimed to have last seen Astor standing beside Archibald Butt near the bridge when the vessel slid beneath the surface, which is borne out by the fact that Astor's crushed and soot-covered body would have been in the area when the forward funnel collapsed and possibly carried him under.

11

WILLIAM THOMAS STEAD

A LAST CRUSADE

I'M GOING to New York, after all, so you'll be in charge about two weeks."

Startled, the assistant editor of England's prestigious *Review of Reviews* replied, "I thought you had decided not to make the trip."

"That was before I received this cable. I would prefer to stay here, but the president of the United States cannot be denied without good reason. This will be my last crusade. I'm too old to be in the thick of another fight. I'll make the round trip on the *Titanic* and return before you know I've gone." Later he confided that he "rather looked forward to a splendid voyage in company with Evangeline Booth," who eight years previously had been placed in command of the Salvation Army in the United States.

William Thomas Stead was known throughout England for having been the moving spirit behind many efforts to bring about change. His most severe critics insisted that he was infamous and a former criminal. "The man is a lunatic," a member of Parliament once said in Commons. The honorable member's castigation of the then-editor of the *Pall Mall Gazette* evoked shouts of approval and hearty applause. Stead's name later became familiar throughout the English-speaking world, but outside of his native land few persons recognized his face.

Since the first-class roster of the maiden voyage of the *Titanic* included many Americans who did not recognize Stead, it was a room steward who first greeted him by name. "For God's sake, keep quiet," the passenger urged. "These American ladies won't know who I am unless you tell them. I'd like to have a little peace and quiet on this trip."

William Thomas Stead had a thirty-year reputation across England as a crusading newspaper editor. He was traveling to New York to speak at the behest of U.S. President William Howard Taft at a peace conference on April 20.

His sudden desire for anonymity—quite unlike him in many respects—was not entirely successful. A handful of ladies looked askance at him when they encountered him on deck or as they dined in the luxurious saloons. These passengers had learned that they were in company with *the* Mr. Stead, but unlike the English travelers, they knew few details about the crusade that had made his name a household word nearly three decades earlier.

BORN AND reared in Northumberland, Stead, son of a Congregational minister, conformed wholly to the customs of the day during his childhood and adolescence. After having worked for a time in the office of a merchant in Newcastle-on-Tyne, he managed to procure a new job. With no training or experience, he became editor of the *Darlington Northern Echo* at the age of twenty-two.

Early in 1880 Stead learned that editor John Morley of the influential *Pall Mall Gazette* was nearing retirement and was seeking an assistant to succeed him. Rushing to London, the man with a glib tongue who had learned by doing was soon established at the *Gazette*.

Stead no sooner took over from Morley than he surprised his readers with a series of innovations. He employed an artist and began running illustrations in the staid old publication. He introduced a feature that was new to British journalism—the interview. As the newspaper's editor, Stead railed against Siberian labor camps, denounced Bulgarian war crimes in the Balkans, and denounced slavery in the Congo. With equal passion he called for reforms in the process by which babies were adopted, increased housing for the poor, and the establishment of public libraries. With circulation inching upward, two years after he became editor Stead launched a carefully prepared crusade. His admirers lauded him for it, but his detractors said that he was interested only in publicity and boosting circulation.

On Monday, July 6, 1885, the *Gazette* appeared with its customary sedate masthead. Underneath, however, longtime subscribers were surprised by the lead story, which began: "The Report of our Secret Commission will be read to-day with a shuddering horror that will thrill throughout the world." Only one person of prominence seems to have cooperated with workers of the "Secret Commission": Evangeline Booth, the London commander of the Salvation Army who had previously held commands in the worst slums of London. The story continued:

Revelations which we begin to publish to-day cannot fail to touch the heart and rouse the conscience of the English people. . . . "Am I my sister's keeper?" That paraphrase of the excuse of CAIN, will not dull the first smart of pain which will be felt by every decent man who learns the kind of atrocities which are being perpetrated in cool blood in the very shadow of our churches and within a stone's throw of our courts. It is a veritable slave trade that is going on around us; but as it takes place in the heart of London, it is a scandal—an outrage on public morality—even to allude to it. We have kept silence too long. . . . The Home, the School, the Church, the Press are silent. The law is actually accessory to crime. Parents culpably neglect even to warn their children of the existence of dangers of which many learn the first time when they have become its prey.

In the second column readers discovered, "The Child-Prostitute of our day is the image into which, with the tacit acquiescence of those who call themselves by His name, men have moulded the form once fashioned in the likeness of GOD." After additional columns of preachments, readers reached a headline reading: THE MAIDEN TRIBUTE OF MODERN BABYLON—THE REPORT OF OUR SECRET COMMISSION.

Stead had gone into London's West End where, with the connivance of staff members, he had purchased for sexual purposes Eliza Armstrong for the sum of five pounds. The thirteen-year-old girl had no idea what was taking place, but the drunken mother who sold her was under no delusions. The impact of this revelation was shattering to the British public. They were justly proud that their nation was "the most enlightened in the entire world concerning that abhorrent institution known as slavery." Many of them derided Americans as "citizens of a nation where it took civil war to do away with slavery." It was an abomination, most aristocrats agreed, for an insufferable and egotistical editor to rage about "white slavery" that he alleged to be flourishing in the heart of the British Empire.

When the *Pall Mall Gazette* completed its account of "The Maiden Tribute of Modern Babylon," no reader doubted that its editor had stirred up a hornet's nest. He offered indisputable proof that child prostitution flourished openly in London, especially in the fashionable West End.

PALL MALL GAZETTE

Stead became the focal point of a moral storm in England when he published an exposé entitled "The Maiden Tribute of Modern Babylon," in which he described how for £5 he was able to purchase the services of Eliza Armstrong (pictured to the left), a thirteen-year-old prostitute.

The authorities reacted vigorously. Stead was arrested and a hearing was scheduled in the city's Old Bailey. The barristers agreed that the editor was in contempt of the criminal law that set the age of consent at fourteen years. Whether or not he violated the underage child he purchased from her mother was beside the point; he had printed reports "that caused every decent citizen to shudder."

In short order, Stead was absolved of having committed any major offense, but he was found guilty of distributing pornography, meaning the *Gazette*. The editor served three months in Holloway Jail but exulted that his one-man crusade led to the passage of the Criminal Law Amendment act, popularly called "Stead's Law," which raised the age of consent to sixteen.

Four years after his release Stead resigned his post to devote his full time to founding a new publication that he called the *Review of Reviews*. His brainchild proved so successful that in 1891 he launched an American edition and the following year began publication in Australia. Stead interviewed Europe's celebrities and political figures and enlarged his own circle of acquaintances, which allowed him to lunch with the Prince of Wales occasionally. Once Stead's Law took effect, the crusader who had rocked an empire fought for and won reforms in the Royal Navy. He was less successful in modifying statutes that reinforced the concept that men are inherently superior to women. His most significant achievement in that area was the placement of numerous women on the staffs of the publications he controlled. Nevertheless, Stead saw his calling as the champion of "oppressed races, ill-treated

HARLAND AND WOLFF

The first-class lounge was the finest ever seen aboard an ocean liner and provided an excellent setting for the kind of intimate or group conversation that Stead enjoyed in enlisting aid for his moral crusades.

animals, underpaid typists, misunderstood women, persecuted parsons, vilified public men, would-be suicides, hot-gospellers of every sort and childless parents."

One newspaper described Stead as "very nearly a great man and certainly a most extraordinary one." His penchant for worthy causes and uprooting corruption led some to compare him to Peter the Hermit, "preaching the Crusades out of his time."

Another of Stead's causes was what the *New York Times* termed "preaching the propaganda of universal peace." His opposition to the Boer War in South Africa brought him to the attention of William Howard Taft. Although the American doubted that much would come of Stead's proposal to form an International Union to Combat Militarism, Taft remembered it when he became president in 1908. This led to a 1912 cable from Washington inviting the editor, age sixty-four, to undertake one more crusade for the cause of world peace and to speak at an international peace conference scheduled to open on April 20. Stead accepted eagerly, then fervently vowed that after having delivered an address at the upcoming conference to be held in New York's Carnegie Hall he would hang up his hat and never get caught up in another crusade of any sort.

ABOARD THE *Titanic* Stead presumably devoted much of his time to revising and polishing the manuscript of his upcoming speech, for few of the survivors recalled anything about his activities aboard ship. Father Thomas Byles was of the opinion that he saw Stead chatting with "American journalist Frank Millet" after the collision when passengers began congregating on deck. He was standing close enough to the pair, he said, to hear Stead end the conversation by saying, "Well, I guess it's nothing of any consequence; I think I'll go back to my cabin and read awhile."

Later, Stead was roused from his cabin by Andrew Cunningham, one of the ship's stewards, and finally consented to wear his life belt. Apparently, he chose not to wear the life belt for long. He was last seen in the first-class smoking lounge thoroughly absorbed in his reading and oblivious to the scene around him. He had become something of a spiritualist in his last years, and as the *Titanic* foundered, he was apparently aware that he would soon be leaving this world for another. The longtime editor and champion of lost causes never moved toward the boat deck or took any action to find safety.

WHEN NEWS of the disaster reached London, newspaper editors searched for firsthand reports. A cable directed to Saint John's, Newfoundland, said that the *Daily Telegraph* was offering one thousand pounds to anyone who could provide the newspaper with an exclusive account of the sinking. In New York the *Times* reported on April 17, "A Marconigram, which it has been impossible to deliver, is addressed to W. T. Stead, once editor of The Review of Reviews, from a big London paper, asking him to Marconi back to them a story of the disaster."

The job of describing the last hours of the *Titanic* and her passengers would have been a good opportunity for Stead to crusade for safety at sea. Unfortunately, the man responsible for having shaken the British Empire with "The Maiden Tribute of Modern Babylon" did not survive the journey to take on a final cause.

12

ISIDOR AND IDA STRAUS

HAND IN HAND

NO OTHER place is quite like the Côte d'Azur," Isidor Straus once confided to his chief subordinates about the area most Americans called the Riviera. "Mrs. Straus and I have taken a look at most of our own spas and resorts and have found them lacking. Newport is elegant and appeals to those who are chiefly interested in high society. But neither Newport nor Hot Springs has olive and citrus trees outlined by perhaps the most beautiful flowers in the world."

Having acquired control of R. H. Macy and Company in 1896, Straus traveled anywhere in the world as he pleased. He became fascinated with the Rhine River after seeing it during his many trips to his factories in Germany, yet he always put the Riviera at the top of his list of vacation destinations.

After one of the most delightful stays he and his wife had ever experienced, they turned their eyes homeward toward New York and booked passage on the *Titanic*. They were assigned to stateroom C 55, two levels below the boat deck. Since their manservant, John Farthing, and their maid, Ellen Bird, accompanied them, the department store magnate was charged about $2,150 for the voyage. The White Star Line did not include Farthing and Bird on its passenger list.

Before the elegant vessel was beyond sight of the Irish coastline, Straus entered the smoking room and struck up a conversation with Col. Archibald Gracie, a retired army officer who both liked and admired the gentleman who was approaching his seventieth birthday. Their conversation had begun while both of them were on deck when the liner left Southampton. They were standing close to the rail when the *Titanic* and the much smaller *New York* were involved in what the military officer termed an "ominous accident."

117

Partly because they liked one another, partly because their staterooms were conveniently close to one another, "From the very beginning to the end of our trip, we were together several times each day," Gracie later wrote. Looking back upon the events of the fateful Sunday night, he remembered discussing with Straus their "jolly well close miss as we got under way."

Straus had commented to Gracie that the Southampton incident was far from his first brush with death. He and his wife had been passengers on the White Star's *Olympic* when it was struck by a vessel of the Royal Navy. With a ram protruding from its bow, the HMS *Hawke* was known to its crew as a "killer ship." Without firing a shot, it could thrust its ram into an enemy vessel and virtually disembowel it. Liners such as the *Olympic* were vulnerable, for the ram of the *Hawke* was heavy enough to penetrate the watertight compartments designed to keep a crippled ship afloat for hours or days.

On September 20, 1911, according to an Admiralty inquiry, the 46,000-ton *Olympic* pulled the 7,000-ton *Hawke* into the liner's wake, forcing the cruiser's ram into the *Olympic*'s stern quarter on the starboard side. When the deadly device was withdrawn from the ocean liner, big piles of its gear and dozens of pieces of luggage could be seen on the deck of the *Hawke*. Although severely damaged, the *Olympic* remained on so nearly an even keel that only those passengers who, like Straus, saw and heard the impact knew that there had been a collision. The accident did not cause potential passengers to worry about booking passage on a ship that was said to be able to withstand anything. Rather, the survival of the *Olympic* almost seven months before the *Titanic* sailed seems to have boosted the impression that nothing could send either White Star liner to the bottom.

Over the course of their conversation, Straus learned that Gracie was keenly interested in the American Civil War and confessed that he had played a part in the conflict. He probably did not mention that in some respects his loyalty still belonged to the defeated South. As recently as 1895 Straus had participated in the fifth annual dinner of the Confederate Veterans of New York and had been seated at the head table with Col. A. G. Dickson, commander of the veterans unit known as a "camp."

According to Gracie's account of the voyage, "About noon Mr. and Mrs. Straus were particularly happy in anticipation of communicating by wireless telegraphy with their son and his wife." Aboard the Hamburg-American liner *Amerika,* Jesse Straus and his wife were headed, not for Europe as Gracie assumed, but for New York and

Isidor and Ida Straus were returning from vacationing on the French Riviera aboard the Titanic. *He had been a blockade-runner during the Civil War, a congressman from New York, an adviser to President Grover Cleveland, part-owner of Macy's, and sometime philanthropist. When he refused to join her in the lifeboat, she relinquished her seat to be with him.*

home. "Some time before six o'clock," Gracie wrote, "full of content-
ment, they told me of the message of greeting received in reply [to
their wireless]." Looking back upon that tranquil evening, Gracie
concluded, "This last good-bye to their loved ones must have been a
consoling thought when the end came a few hours thereafter."

After dinner Sunday evening, Gracie and many other first-class
passengers found places in the Palm Room where they could listen
to "the always delightful music of the *Titanic*'s band while sipping
coffee from cups of bone china." On such occasions, Gracie noted,
"full dress was always required, and it was a subject both of observation and admiration, that there were so many beautiful women
aboard the ship."

The Strauses, however, retired to their cabin, and he finished
reading a book on the battle of Chickamauga written by Gracie.
After the collision the couple seem to have remained in their stateroom until the stewards awakened the passengers with news of the
accident and the captain's decision to abandon ship. Both then
went on deck about 1:10 A.M., where Gracie found them "chatting quite cheerily." He offered to lead Mrs. Straus to the boats,
but she declined even when her husband urged her to go. Later
both of them went to lifeboat number eight, which was being
loaded on the port side of the boat deck. Precisely what then took
place is uncertain, for eyewitnesses gave slightly divergent
accounts. John R. Joyce, a New Mexico banker who had offices on
Fifth Avenue and who was a passenger on the *Carpathia*, told *New
York Times* reporters that the survivors were awed by the conduct
of the Strauses. His account was corroborated by Mrs. Paul Schu-
bert of Derby, Connecticut, whose stateroom was near that of the
elderly couple.

Accompanied by their maid, the Strauses stepped up to boat
number eight. Pushing her maid forward so that she would be the
first of the trio to enter the lifeboat, Ida Straus passed either a
blanket or her fur coat to Ellen. Crew members were shouting at
the top of their voices, "Women and children first!" Visibly strain-
ing, Ida managed to get started up the four-foot gunwale, struggling to surmount it. A member of the crew noticed her husband's
advanced age and gestured for him to follow his wife. London
businessman Hugh Woolner stepped to the side of Straus when he
did not move and said he was sure that "no one would protest if
an old gentleman broke the unwritten law of the sea."

"I will not go before the other men," Straus responded as he
turned away from the lifeboat still being loaded and not yet having

Eighteen-year-old Isidor Straus was too young to fight for the Confederacy, and so he became a purchasing agent for the South and traveled to England and back via blockade-runners similar to the one pictured above.

started its long descent to the water below. Ida Straus, who saw and heard what took place on the deck, managed to rejoin her husband. "We will not be separated," she said firmly. "As we have lived together, so will we die together." Joining hands, husband and wife turned their backs upon safety, walked calmly to their stateroom, and were never seen alive again.

BORN IN Bavaria in 1845, Isidor Straus immigrated to America at nine years of age to join his mother and father who had settled in Talbotton, Georgia. Perhaps his eagerness to be admitted to West Point—an ambition in which he failed—helped to attract him to Archibald Gracie. The recollections of the military officer indicate that Straus spoke frequently of his early experiences, which included volunteering to fight for the Confederacy.

After he enlisted, the men of his company voted to make Straus one of their lieutenants, but his commission never came. According to the *New York Times,* "The Confederacy did not have the guns to arm its men, and wanted no boys." Thus sixteen-year-old Straus returned home and with his parents soon moved to Columbus, Georgia. From that city, he made his first west-to-east crossing of the Atlantic.

MACY'S DEPARTMENT STORE

The grieving employees of Macy's Department Store funded a memorial to the Strauses, which was erected at Broadway and West 106th Street.

In 1863 the Confederate Department of State requested a Columbus firm to send someone to England to purchase ships. Partly, perhaps, because of his European background and partly because most men were in uniform, eighteen-year-old Straus was chosen to serve as a purchasing agent. With ships of the Federal blockade hovering close to every major port in the South, young Straus took passage on a small, fast blockade-runner and managed to reach England. There is no record that he succeeded in purchasing even one vessel for the Confederacy, but he never forgot that turbulent era and frequently spoke of it.

At war's end he discussed with his father the advisability of moving to a major city to get a customer base for a mercantile operation. They considered Philadelphia but settled upon New York. Organizing the firm of L. Straus and Son, they began importing "earthware" and were successful enough by 1874 to be operating the china and glassware department of R. H. Macy and Company. Isidor and his brother Nathan gained Macy partnerships in 1888 and less than a decade later purchased full ownership of the huge store. By that time Straus factories were scattered throughout much of Europe, necessitating frequent transoceanic voyages.

After having served as New York's commissioner on the New York and New Jersey bridge commission, Straus visited Washington and helped persuade President Grover Cleveland to call a special session of Congress to address the fiscal crisis of 1893. Entering politics, the one-time Confederate agent won a seat in the U.S. House of Representatives and a place on its Ways and Means Committee. He became so heavily involved in Cleveland's campaign for a second term that he gave up all thought of political office for himself.

CHIEF OFFICER Henry T. Wilde, at least momentarily in command at the lifeboat approached by the Strauses, was distraught and somewhat confused by the ponderous davits that controlled the small craft. As Isidor and Ida Straus disappeared from view, Wilde hastily herded a group of about twenty women aft and instructed them to climb into lifeboat number ten. As a result of that impulsive action, number eight began its descent to the sea when it was less than half filled—occupied only by twenty-six passengers and two crew members.

A few days later, a brief *Times* tribute to the Strauses included a summary informing readers that "in their accounts of the conduct of the officers and crew and of the passengers at the time of the disaster, not a man or woman who came ashore last night had a word of anything but praise. The crew is said to have acted with a calmness which might have characterized their actions were they merely going through a practice drill."

Erroneous as that news report was, it remained true that crew members did succeed in getting most women from first class off the doomed liner. In addition to Mrs. Straus, only four others perished: Mrs. H. J. Allison of Montreal and her daughter, Miss A. E. Isham of New York, and Miss Edith Evans—whose full name was not on the passenger list but was supplied by Gracie, who identified her as a friend of the Strauses. Among second-class passengers, the story was different, and among steerage passengers the death toll was horrible. Gracie later waxed enthusiastic about the fact that so few women from first class were lost. This fact, he wrote "is in itself the most sublime tribute that could be paid to the self-sacrifice and gallantry of the first cabin men." He wrote nothing about women from second class and steerage.

ON APRIL 16, 1912, the *New York Times* described Straus as "a supporter of almost every philanthropic and charitable institution in New York, regardless of creed." His body was later recovered and buried first at Beth-El Cemetery in Brooklyn and then moved to Woodlawn Cemetery in the Bronx, but his wife's body was never found.

At the time of the sinking of the *Titanic,* Nathan Straus, Isidor's brother, was in the Hotel Russe in Rome recuperating from an illness. On the advice of his physicians, authorities and hotel personnel were careful to keep the news of the disaster from him. His wife sent a cablegram, news of which was given space in the *New York Times,* to their son informing him that his father was gaining strength but must not yet learn of Isidor's death.

Nathan recuperated and soon took over Macy's, but for the rest of his life he mourned his brother and sister-in-law who should not have died when the *Titanic* went down. He served as park commissioner for New York City and as president of its board of health. In that capacity he led a very early crusade for pasteurization of milk. In 1923 Isidor's still-grieving brother was voted "the citizen who has done most for public welfare in the first quarter century of greater New York's history." Retiring from business just three years after the *Titanic* disaster, Nathan Straus turned Macy's over to his nephew and Isidor's son, Jesse Isidor—who exchanged wireless messages with his parents only a few hours before they took the steps that caused them to be hailed as "sweethearts in death."

13

HARRY WIDENER

A WISH FULFILLED

CAN I describe Harry Widener for your readers in one sentence?" mused a lifelong friend in response to a question from a Philadelphia reporter. "Absolutely not. He was a very complex person. He spent a fortune on rare books, but he was in no sense a traditional bibliophile. He had many interests and excelled at all of them. I suppose my own most vivid impression of Harry is that a new acquaintance could spend half a day with him and never guess that Harry stood to inherit Philadelphia's largest fortune. He was totally unassuming, unpretentious, and never put on airs of any sort."

The subject of that informal eulogy, one of the thirty-two Philadelphians who went down with the *Titanic*, had gone to England in March 1912. He wanted a few weeks to prowl about London before his parents joined him. George B. and Eleanor Widener were planning to come to assemble a trousseau for their daughter, also named Eleanor. They'd go about the chore leisurely, and all three could return on the maiden voyage of the finest ocean liner ever built.

Described in the *New York Times* as "one of the nation's foremost financiers," George B. Widener had always allowed his son to spend freely whenever he spotted something he wanted. Since he was still in his twenties, reasoned the father, Harry might become resentful if he had to wait to inherit his fortune. "Take plenty of time looking," he advised. "Check as carefully as you can. When you've done that after having found something you want, get it."

Thus Harry, who had acquired his love of books at Harvard, selected Dr. A. W. S. Rosenbach to serve as his agent when the contents of a fine Antwerp library were scheduled to be auctioned in London. Rosenbach procured only one treasure for him—a first folio of Shakespeare's works. Both the *Illustrated London News* and

Harry Elkins Widener was a great lover of books. He specialized in nineteenth-century English authors and had an avid interest also in well-illustrated volumes. His father and he were lost with the Titanic, *but his mother survived. She allegedly claimed that Harry was with her but surrendered his place in the lifeboat to fetch a recently purchased rare volume of Francis Bacon's essays.*

HARVARD UNIVERSITY LIBRARY

the London *Times* reported the sale price of £18,000 as the highest ever paid for such a work. Later, when part of the well-known Hoe Library was assembled in New York for an auction, Harry attended and acquired several minor pieces. He returned to Philadelphia disappointed that his bid of forty-nine thousand dollars for a Gutenberg Bible had been topped by railroad magnate Henry E. Huntington. Having booked passage for England on the liner *Mauretania,* Widener wrote to Walter M. Hill of Chicago that he would be back in New York for the second part of the Hoe auction. He did not expect to get much of significance there, he wrote, as Huntington seemed bent on capturing the most valuable items and he "didn't care to take the leavings."

In London, Harry was in and out of Sotheby's auction house for several weeks and through Rosenbach acquired a 1598 collection of essays by the English philosopher-scientist Francis Bacon. Although not regarded by collectors as being in the same class as the Gutenberg Bible, the small book was prized by its new owner. Talking one evening with the collector Bernard Quaritch, Harry exhibited his purchase and remarked, "I think I'll take that little Bacon with me in my pocket." Laughingly, he added, "If I am shipwrecked on the *Titanic* it will go with me."

An admirer of Robert Louis Stevenson, Widener often carried a copy of *Treasure Island* with him when he traveled. His admiration for

Stevenson was so great that he had completed arrangements to have Stevenson's *Memoirs* privately printed before he sailed on the *Mauretania*. Widener's collection, housed at Lynwood Hall in suburban Philadelphia, also included a 1613 edition of Sir Philip Sidney's *Arcadia* and a volume of William Cowper's poems that was once owned by novelist William Makepeace Thackeray. He told collector A. Edward Newton, "I do not care to be remembered merely as a collector of a few books, however fine. My fervent wish is that anything I accumulate may some day be connected with a great library."

Widener had been aboard the *Titanic* only a few hours before he browsed the liner's library, reporting to his parents that he found the collection to have been surprisingly well chosen, but he spent little time there. Far younger than most men in first class, he was with one or both of his parents much of the time.

As a matter of course, Harry was in attendance when his parents hosted the informal reception for Captain Smith on Sunday evening. The senior Widener had chosen a splendid champagne for the occasion, but Smith declined a glass. Executives of the White Star Line were very strict, he pointed out. While at sea an officer was forbidden to touch alcohol in any form.

Although no survivor of the disaster said anything about the necklace Eleanor Widener wore for the reception, it is impossible to believe that anyone who glanced at her could have failed to notice it. A dispatch from London informed the *New York Times* on April 18 that the queen of Philadelphia society had taken three pearl necklaces with her. A special insurance policy for $750,000 that covered them reportedly included an unusual clause. For the coverage to be valid, Mrs. Widener must wear each of the three necklaces during her five-day voyage to New York.

Survivors remembered seeing Harry only two or three times after the reception. About ten o'clock he was noticed sitting at a card table with Archibald Butt, Clarence Moore, and William Carter. Three hours later he reportedly helped his father to seat his mother in lifeboat number four, after which both men stepped back. John B. Thayer and his son Jack—also from Philadelphia—assisted Mrs. Thayer into the same boat, after which they too moved away.

Second Officer Lightoller, to whom Captain Smith had delegated oversight of the lifeboats, gave a different account of the last glimpse of the Philadelphians whom he knew by sight. In formal testimony before a board of inquiry, he said he was the last person to see the Widener men:

I stuck to the ship until the water came up to my ankles. There had been no lamentations, no demonstrations either from the the men passengers as they saw the last lifeboats go, and there was no wailing or crying, no outburst from the men who lined the ship's rail as the *Titanic* gave clear signals that she was about to go under.

The men stood quietly as if they were in church. They knew that they were in the sight of God; that in a moment judgment would be passed upon them. Finally, the ship took a dive, reeling for a moment, then plunging. I was sucked to the side of the ship against the grating over the blower for the exhaust. There was an explosion. It blew me to the surface again, only to be sucked back again by the water rushing into the ship.

This time I landed against the grating over the pipes which furnish a draught for the funnels, and stuck there. There was another explosion, and I came to the surface. The ship seemed to be heaving tremendous sighs as she went down. I found myself not many feet from the ship, but on the other side. The ship had turned around while I was under the water.

I came up near a collapsible [Englehardt] boat and grabbed it. Many men were in the water near me. They had jumped at the last minute. A funnel came within four inches of me and killed one of the swimmers. Thirty clung to the capsized boat, and a life-boat, with forty survivors in it already, finally took them off.

George D. Widener and Harry Elkins Widener were among those who jumped at the last minute. So did Robert Williams Daniel. The three of them went down together. Daniel struck out, lashing the water with his arms until he had made a point far distant from the sinking monster of the sea. Later he was picked up by one of the passing life-boats. The Wideners were not seen again.

A dispatch of April 16 from Philadelphia to the *Times* reported that as of midnight on Tuesday, nearly all of the thirty-three persons from the City of Brotherly Love known to be aboard the liner had been accounted for. In addition to the father-son Widener pair, attorney William C. Dulles was believed to be dead. The name of J. R. McGough had not been found among lists of survivors, but it was hoped that a "James Geough" on one list or another would prove to be the toy buyer for Gimbel Brothers who made

On Sunday night, April 14, the Wideners hosted a reception for Captain Smith, recognizing his years of service to the White Star Line and his impending retirement. The captain was fond of the Wideners and was pleased to attend, but he excused himself at 9 p.m. to get back to the running of the ship.

his home in Philadelphia. T. D. M. Cardeza was reported to have been saved, but his valet, Louis Gustave, was considered to be dead, as was George Widener's valet, Edward Keeping.

Peter A. B. Widener, patriarch of the family that included the youthful book collector, was too agitated to stay at home. Despite his advanced years, he set out for New York "to take personal charge of a search by wireless for news of the safety" of his brother and nephew—who were initially misidentified as his son and grandson. Although he was not successful on the morning of April 17, he continued his quest and told reporters that "he would not give up his kin as lost until the last steamship which responded to

As a cartoonist eerily pointed out, one in three passengers aboard the Titanic *survived the crisis.*

the signals of the Titanic had disembarked its last passenger, either at an American or a European port." At the offices of the White Star Line, Widener "was deeply affected when told that while Mrs. Widener was among the saved, neither his brother's nor his nephew's name appeared on the list of survivors sent out by Capt. Rostron of the Carpathia."

As a memorial to her bibliophile son, Eleanor Widener made an unrestricted gift to Harvard University to establish the Harry Elkins Widener Library. On June 24, 1915, newspapers reported the opening of "the world's largest college library," a fitting tribute to Harry, the youngest man in first class to die when the "unsinkable" *Titanic* went down.

In the center of the library, on the mezzanine between the first and second floors, is the Harry Elkins Widener Memorial Room. It contains Widener's personal collection of thirty-five hundred rare books, focusing largely on nineteenth-century English authors and nineteenth-century illustrated books.

One of the great legends of Harvard University is that a condition of the Widener donation required all Harvard men to pass a swimming test before graduation, believing that had Harry been able to swim he might not have died when the *Titanic* sank. The swimming requirement, however, dated from a time when the U.S. Navy had men attending Harvard, and the notion that Harry Widener might have lived had he been able to swim ignores the fact that the cold temperature of the North Atlantic caused most of the *Titanic*'s fatalities as the passengers in the water succumbed to hypothermia.

14

BENJAMIN GUGGENHEIM

BLACK SHEEP

AMONG THE tales of the wealthy Americans aboard the *Titanic*, Benjamin Guggenheim's story presents the most unanswered questions. Like most others in first class, he boarded at Southampton, but there is no record that he traveled there via the boat train from London. The *Titanic*'s passenger list suggests that he sailed alone, but many people remembered having seen him with a woman. It was rumored after the sinking that he had his mistress along, but it is impossible to discover who she was—if, indeed, she existed.

Logan Marshall began trying to assemble the story of the liner and her passengers within months after she went down. His study, *The Sinking of the Titanic*, published in 1912, asserted that a steward whom he identified only as Johnson served the area that included Guggenheim's cabin. According to Johnson, as reported by Marshall, the wealthy American had a male secretary with him. Realizing that the ship would stay afloat only a short time longer after it had struck the iceberg, said Johnson, Guggenheim donned a dress suit and instructed his secretary to do the same thing so that both of them could die like gentlemen.

"I won't go down like a beast," Guggenheim is quoted as having said in Johnson's presence. "I will go to my death like a man." Then, turning to the steward, he reportedly gave him instructions: "Tell my wife, Johnson, if I don't make it that I played my cards straight and to the end. She must know that I wouldn't let a single woman be left aboard this vessel because Ben Guggenheim played the coward. Tell her that my last thoughts and memories will be centered upon her and our three daughters, but that I considered it my duty as a gentleman to reserve the lifeboats for the women and children." Johnson claimed that Guggenheim and

Hardly a picture of conservative respectability, Benjamin Guggenheim had been with his mistress abroad, and they were returning to New York on the Titanic.

ILLUSTRATED LONDON NEWS

his secretary then "sauntered to the upper deck and began calmly talking with Major Butt and Colonel Astor."

Marshall clearly believed this story, versions of which have appeared in numerous newspapers. In the years since, many have questioned if Guggenheim's so-called secretary might have been his mistress dressed as a man.

To complicate the story, documents held by other members of the Guggenheim clan indicate that Benjamin probably had his valet, Victor Giglio, with him. It would have been easy for Johnson—if that was the correct name of the steward—to mistake a valet for a male secretary. Yet no Giglio is listed among the first-class, second-class, or third-class passengers who boarded at Southampton, Cherbourg, or Queenstown. If a mistress disguised as a valet or a secretary was with Guggenheim, there are no records confirming this person's presence aboard the *Titanic.*

GUGGENHEIM'S FATHER, Meyer, had emigrated from Switzerland to the United States in 1847 at the age of nineteen. Aboard ship to his new home, he met Barbara Myers and soon made her his wife. They had seven sons.

Penniless upon debarking, the immigrant got his start by peddling shoelaces on the streets of Philadelphia, but he soon became a prosperous importer of Swiss embroideries. In 1887 his career took a sudden turn when friends interested him in copper mining in Colorado. In 1888 the Guggenheims—all of Meyer's sons were

VINCENT ASTOR'S GRIEF

Son of John Jacob Offers a Fortune for Word of His Father.

WIDENER WORRIES OVER SON

Mrs. B. Guggenheim Blames Company for Shortage of Lifeboats.

As soon as word of the disaster reached New York, Guggenheim's widow, Fioretta, visited the White Star Line offices. When it became apparent that her husband was not among the survivors, she was heard to ask why there were not enough boats for the passengers and crew.

involved in the business—built a copper smelter at Pueblo, Colorado, and gradually invested in other mining ventures. By 1901 they controlled the American Smelting and Refining Company, the leading company of the industry. They took over gold mines in Alaska, tin and nitrate mines in South America, and rubber plantations in Africa.

Benjamin or one of his older brothers persuaded their father to develop closer ties with mine operators and then to form the Guggenheim Exploration Company. Radical to the extreme when it began business in 1899, the exploration company "combined in itself the characteristics of prospector, engineer, promoter, and financial backer." As a result, "Every new discovery of ore in any part of the world brought a Guggenheim representative to the spot, ready to finance the prospecting, construct the engineering works, and manage a flotation of stock."

According to the *New York Times*, Benjamin masterminded a complex set of moves that won control of the American Smelting and Refining Company for the family. "Having seen the great object [or takeover] an actuality, Benjamin Guggenheim went to Europe for a well-earned rest," the newspaper reported.

Upon his return to the United States, Benjamin went to Milwaukee and built a large plant for the manufacture of mining equipment. After three profitable years, it merged with the International

Steam Pump Company, and Guggenheim promptly became chairman of the executive committee and then president, placing him at the head of an organization with seven plants in the United States, one in England, and a workforce of ten thousand men.

Severing many ties with his family and becoming its "black sheep," Guggenheim established offices in London and Paris and began making plans for expansion of his International Steam Pump Company. It was this company's business that took him to Europe in January 1912, and he was returning home on the *Titanic*. No first-class survivor corroborated the story told by "Johnson," so when and how the international financier died remains a mystery.

NO CLOUD of doubt hangs over the reactions of his wife and one of his brothers to the news of his loss at sea. In New York, the *Times* detailed the activities of Benjamin's wife, Fioretta:

> About 10 o'clock [on the morning of April 17], just when the crowd in the office [of the White Star Line] was largest, Mrs. Benjamin Guggenheim arrived, accompanied by her brother and sister-in-law, Mr. and Mrs. De Witt F. Seligman. Mrs. Guggenheim gave every evidence of great mental agitation. Although she bore up bravely, it was apparent that the terrible suspense was threatening a complete breakdown.
>
> Like all the others who were there Mrs. Guggenheim carefully went over the lists supplied by the company and questioned several of the clerks. Then when she found that there was no message of hope for her, she sank down on a bench. She talked freely with the newspaper men, seeking from them every bit of information she could obtain about the disaster.
>
> "If so many were lost then the White Star Line did not have enough boats," declared Mrs. Guggenheim passionately. "There should have been more boats."

Questioned about the last hours of the industrialist, Sen. Simon Guggenheim of Colorado responded: "Judging from the reports that women and children were put into the boats first, I suppose that my brother was one of those left behind. But I know nothing definite."

If Mrs. Guggenheim knew anything about a companion of her husband, she said nothing. On April 18 she returned for another

It was not long before several newspaper artists latched onto the shortage of lifeboats as the chief cause for the high death toll in the Titanic *disaster.*

fruitless round of seeking and questioning. By the time Fioretta Guggenheim abandoned hope some time during the following week, whispers about the mysterious companion of her husband were already afloat in the world's financial centers. Was the man who had distanced himself from his brothers traveling alone, or did he have a companion? If an unidentified man or woman was with him, what was that person's role?

These questions point to larger ones that will never be answered satisfactorily. No one knows the name of every victim and every survivor of the *Titanic*. Rich and famous passengers and their coterie showed so little interest in members of the crew that names of stewards, engineers, firemen, stokers, and other seamen were not listed in any major newspaper of the period. Compiled much later from White Star Line records, lists of crew members are known to be full of errors. Thus it is impossible to determine with certainty which of the approximately eight hundred workers aboard the *Titanic* perished and which of them survived.

Evidence from several sources strongly suggests that some professional gamblers were aboard but were using assumed names, so their identities cannot be traced. Neither is it possible to find out how many stowaways slipped aboard at the ship's three ports of call, or who they were. Strangely from today's viewpoint, passenger lists cite numerous enigmatic references to valets and maids whose names were not recorded and who can be identified only from the records of their employers. A few of these "mystery passengers" probably escaped, but the majority most likely did not find places in the *Titanic*'s lifeboats.

Within days after Guggenheim's distraught widow assailed the management of the *Titanic* about its insufficient lifeboats, they became a subject of intense investigation. In the United States her opinion was accepted, but an English board of inquiry concluded that the British owners of the *Titanic* "had adhered to the letter of the law [concerning lifeboats] and hence were blameless."

15

MAGGIE BROWN

UNSINKABLE!

WHAT CLASS, madam?"

"First, of course. I have three crates of art objects in addition to my luggage," Mrs. James J. Brown informed the White Star Line's ticket agent, drawing herself up to her full height so that her body language clearly signaled that she would never think of traveling in a second-class compartment.

"I can give you a stateroom on B Deck, forward. That will be $130, American. Your art objects will have to go as cargo, but I am sure you know that the *Titanic* has space to spare."

"So I have heard, but my antiquities must have special care," responded the Denver, Colorado, woman as she handed over her fare. "These crates cannot be treated as ordinary cargo."

"Certainly not, madam; I will give you receipts for each of them. The *Titanic* is lying at anchor, so you may board by the next tender."

The buxom passenger who often said of herself, "The only small parts of my body are my hands and my feet," accepted her ticket and claim checks with a shiver. At Cherbourg, France, the sky had become overcast during the early afternoon. Sitting next to another American aboard the tender, she spontaneously turned to her and said, "I'm Mrs. J. J. Brown of Denver, but I hope that long before our voyage is over you will be calling me Maggie; everyone else does."

"I'm from Philadelphia," her new acquaintance replied. "My husband, Dr. Bucknell, founded Bucknell University, you know." Gesturing to her seatmate, she continued, "This is Dr. Arthur Jackson Brewe who has done a great deal of important scientific research, you know."

Leaning far forward, Maggie graciously extended her left hand to the scientist, then gestured toward the young woman sitting beside him. "Your daughter, I presume; I believe she must resemble her father rather than you."

Mrs. Bucknell turned faintly pink and answered, "It would be very strange if she resembled me; this young woman is my maid."

Soon the Philadelphians and their new friend who seemed too young to have a pronounced dowager hump were aboard the *Titanic*. With the European season just beginning, Maggie had not planned to go home until many weeks later. On a leisurely journey through much of Europe and part of North Africa, she had acquired less than half of the quantity of fine art she had hoped that the Denver museum would put on exhibition. There would be an afternoon tea at its opening, of course, and logic said she would be invited to serve as hostess. Such an event would almost certainly boost her into a level of society that so far had been closed to her, despite her husband's fortune from copper and gold.

An urgent message that caught up with her "somewhere in the Alps," however, had radically altered her plans. Her young grandson, Pat Palmer, was seriously ill. That gave her no choice but to cut her tour short. Hastily supervising the packing of the "antiquities" purchased in Egypt and Europe, she headed for Cherbourg knowing that the elegant new *Titanic* would call there in a few days. She also knew the vessel promised an Atlantic crossing in only six days. From New York, she could take a fast train that would enable her to be at the bedside of her grandson as quickly as possible. Despite her protestations, had nothing else been available, Maggie would have accepted a second-class cabin. Fortunately, such bourgeois travel would not be necessary for her.

To look at the passenger who was decked out in her personal version of Parisian finery, no one in first class would have guessed that Maggie had grown up in poverty or that when she hit Denver, members of established society assured one another, "Her airs deceive no one; rich or not, she's just a ditch digger's daughter."

Although not quite accurate, that characterization was close to the truth. Margaret Tobin was born July 18, 1867, in a tiny frame house in Hannibal, Missouri. John Tobin, her father, was employed by the Hannibal Gas Works as a laborer. Little Margaret always answered to the nickname Maggie and was never referred to as Molly until after her death.

Maggie Brown was a simple country girl who had married a miner and then struck it rich in Colorado. Denver high society, however, chose not to welcome her, and so Maggie went east to polish her manners and returned with the legend of being "unsinkable."

The ship's veranda café was exactly the kind of setting Maggie Brown enjoyed for enlarging her circle of acquaintances. Gregarious and outspoken, she always found someone to talk to wherever she went.

Having spent her first seventeen years close to the Mississippi River, Maggie meandered far to the west and landed in Leadville, Colorado, a silver mining boom town, where she found work as a seamstress. This was a rough-and-ready place frequented by the likes of the James brothers, Bat Masterson, and Wyatt Earp. Trudging through the muddy streets, she almost certainly saw Doc Holliday more than once before his death in 1887.

Maggie, however, was more interested in J. J. Brown, who had wandered through innumerable played-out gold fields before settling in Leadville as foreman of a small silver mine. Her bright red hair and sparkling blue eyes soon brought her to the attention of the Pennsylvania native who at first sight correctly guessed that she must be "another Irish Catholic like me." Their off-and-on relationship led to marriage in 1890. The newlyweds lived in a two-room log cabin on Iron Hill, close to the mine in which the bridegroom worked.

In time, J. J. moved up the ladder and became superintendent of the Consolidated Mining Company, but the couple's newfound prosperity did not last. The price of silver sank, and this cost the majority of Leadville's workers their jobs. Gold shot upward while silver spiraled downward, so Maggie encouraged J. J., by then with the Ibex Mining Company, to persuade his boss to invest in expanding the Little Jonny mine.

High-grade copper was found early in the renewed exploration, and a seam called "the world's richest gold vein" followed. Thanks to the Little Jonny, by 1894 J. J. and Maggie were rich enough to abandon Leadville in favor of Denver. They found an elegant home in the Capitol Hill section of the city, and Maggie set out to become a member of high society. Commenting upon her efforts, a writer for the *Denver Times* said that no other twenty-seven-year-old in memory "spent more time or money becoming 'civilized' than has Mrs. Brown." Designer dresses made in Paris did not seem to Denver's elite to make up for the coyote heads mounted in Maggie's front hall. Even the acquisition of the 240-acre Avoca ranch south of the city, soon the site of many dinners and balls, made little difference to "Denver's 400."

No one ever questioned Maggie's bulldog tenacity, however. If Denver was not ready to accept her as she was, she seemed to have reasoned, a quite different Mrs. J. J. Brown might make the grade. So she wintered in New York, where she mastered the rudiments of drama and literature at the Carnegie Institute. Then she spent a season in Paris and was tutored in French, the language of refinement at the time.

ON THE fateful Sunday evening in 1912, Maggie, an avid reader, wanted to finish a book she had started earlier on the voyage. "I stretched out on the brass bed [of my stateroom not far from the bow of the *Titanic*]," she said afterward. "[I was] so completely absorbed in my reading [that] I gave little thought to the crash that struck at my window overhead and threw me to the floor. Picking myself up, I proceeded to see what the steamer had struck. On emerging from the stateroom, I found many men in the gangway in their pajamas. All seemed to be quietly listening, thinking nothing serious had occurred, though realizing at the time that the engines had stopped immediately after the crash and the boat was at a standstill."

She later learned that her memory was faulty. The momentum of the *Titanic* moving at or close to her top speed was so great that, though damaged, she continued to plow through the calm icy water long after the iceberg was hit. Returning to her stateroom and her book, Maggie soon heard what she described as "increasing confusion in the hall."

"I again looked out," she remembered, "and saw a man whose face was blanched, his eyes protruding, wearing the look of a haunted creature. He was grasping for breath, and in an undertone he gasped, 'Get your life-saver.' "

On deck Maggie found several of her newest acquaintances. One of them, Mrs. Bucknell of Philadelphia, seemed agitated and confused, so Maggie saw her safely loaded into a lifeboat. She then found that her study of French was to pay an unexpected dividend. A Belgian woman, whose babbling was incomprehensible to the crew, was insisting that she must go below to retrieve her jewelry. Maggie persuaded her to forget her finery and get into the boat before she went "to see what was being done with the boats on the other side [of the liner]."

Silently pondering whether or not she might have to take to the water, knowing herself to be a strong swimmer, she later insisted that she never felt any fear for her own safety. While she was weighing her options, a person she never saw clearly seized her and said, "You are going too," and shoved her into lifeboat number six. By the time the craft completed its long drop to the water below, she had counted "about 14 women in the boat and one man." Second Officer Lightoller later said that Maggie's count was wrong. According to him, he followed the captain's instructions and placed two members of the crew in each boat. Frederick Fleet, the lookout who gave the first danger signal, was one of the men in number six. The other, Lightoller recalled, was Quartermaster Robert Hitchens. A third man joined the lifeboat when one of the women called up that there was only one seaman in the boat, and Lightoller dispatched Maj. Arthur Godfrey Peuchen to climb down into the lifeboat before it reached the water.

Maggie seems never to have identified Fleet, but her lifeboat had not been in the water long before Hitchens attracted her scornful attention. "He was shivering like an aspen," she said. Soon the quartermaster "burst out in a frightened voice, and warned us

A passenger aboard the Carpathia *photographed one of* Titanic's *lifeboats approaching the ship. The survivors had been in the boats for almost four hours. Maggie Brown was in boat number six.*

of the fate that awaited us, telling us our task in rowing away from the sinking ship was futile, as she was so large that in sinking she would take everything for miles around down with her suction."

Maggie said that she seized an oar and signaled for another woman to do so also. "As we pulled away from the boat, we heard sounds of firing," she afterward insisted, "and were told that it was from officers shooting as they were letting down the boats from the steamer, trying to prevent those [steerage passengers] from the lower decks [from] jumping into the lifeboats."

When the liner went under shortly after 2:20 A.M., there was no suction effect. Instead, after a sudden rift in the water, "the sea opened up and the surface foamed like giant arms spread around the ship, and the vessel disappeared from sight, and not a sound was heard."

Soon the mutual dislike between Maggie and Hitchens erupted into the open. Enabled to "fan the air with his hands" since he was not pulling an oar, the quartermaster began "telling us we were likely to drift for days. He forcibly impressed upon us that there was no water in the casks in the lifeboat and no bread, no compass and no chart."

More than two hours after having heard these doleful pronouncements, Maggie said she saw a flash of light. Hitchens dismissed it as being a falling star, but he was soon proved to be wrong. That light came from the *Carpathia.*

Aboard the rescue ship, Maggie's proficiency in French proved a godsend to immigrants who spoke no English. In addition to interpreting for many of them, she helped to compile lists of survivors before collecting money as a present for the *Carpathia*'s crew. Many of them had worked around the clock for more than two days, so first-class survivors readily contributed. By the time the ship docked at New York, nearly ten thousand dollars had been pledged.

White Star Line officials had taken unusual pains to bar photographers from the area in which relatives waited for the arrival of survivors—or news that they would never come—in rows arranged alphabetically by surname. Several reporters managed to elude the security guards, however, and descended upon Maggie as soon as she stepped from the gangplank. They shouted questions about how she managed to survive the tragedy.

"Typical Brown luck," she reputedly told them. "We're unsinkable."

Within days, the woman who had failed to reach the inner circle of Denver's high society was a national and international celebrity. Once comfortably established in Denver's Brown Palace Hotel, she readily met with reporters and photographers. Some of them were so awed by her story that their newspapers devoted entire pages to the account of her heroism and survival. Later she lent her support to the movement seeking women's suffrage.

After her death in 1942 in New York City, her famous one-liner, "We're unsinkable," combined with the false claim about the *Titanic* combined to inspire the Broadway musical, *The Unsinkable Molly Brown.* The show's playwright, Meredith Willson, seems to have used the name Molly because he considered it more musical. The successful 1960 musical was translated to the big screen in 1964, and Debbie Reynolds, who played Molly, was nominated for an Academy Award. The actress praised the woman she portrayed as "a female ahead of her time," saying "Thank you, Molly Brown, for being you! You must have had great fun and joy in life."

16

J. BRUCE ISMAY

SCAPEGOAT

Mrs. HENRY B. FRICK, wife of the American steel magnate, slipped on a wet deck and sprained her ankle while on a short cruise to Madeira. She was so uncomfortable during the first week of April 1912 that she told her husband, "You know I have my heart set on the *Titanic*. Everyone says it will be simply marvelous—but I'm just not up to it." Ten days later, she and her husband rejoiced at "the Providential injury" that saved them from being aboard the liner.

The Fricks' cancellation left open Suite B 52-54-56, complete with a private promenade. Reassigned to J. Pierpont Morgan, it again came open when Morgan sent a message from near Chartres, France, saying, "Business will deny me the pleasure of being one of the first to cross on the finest vessel of the IMM." Mr. and Mrs. J. Horace Harding, who were assigned to B52 for at least twenty-four hours, canceled in order to leave earlier, crossing on the *Mauretania*. Thus the luxurious quarters went to J. Bruce Ismay.

The executive head of the International Merchantile Marine and in 1912 estimated to be worth forty million pounds, Ismay drove to Southampton from his London home in his huge Daimler Landaulette auto. His wife and their three younger children were given a private tour of the liner. Ismay's secretary, W. H. Harrison, took the boat train with his employer's valet, Richard Fry. Since both Ismay and Harrison were traveling on company business, they paid no fare for passage on the *Titanic*. Fry appeared on the passenger list simply as "manservant."

As the eldest son of a shipping magnate, J. Bruce grew up in luxury. After completing his education and taking the leisurely Grand Tour trip that was then a rite of passage for young men of

J. Bruce Ismay had been educated in the most exclusive preparatory schools in England before joining his father's White Star Line and then succeeding him as director in 1899. Over cigars and brandy one night in 1907, he and the chairman of the board of Harland and Wolff sketched out the plans for the three ships of the Olympic *class, which included the* Titanic.

his social standing, he worked for a few years in the New York office of the White Star Line before becoming a partner in his father's firm. Upon the death of the senior Ismay, he took over and was soon persuaded to sell to J. Pierpont Morgan's IMM and become its president at a salary of one hundred thousand dollars per year. In his new role, Ismay was the chief decisionmaker not only for White Star, but also for the Leyland, Dominion, and Atlantic Transport lines, the International Navigation Company, and half a dozen small lines.

It was Ismay who persuaded Morgan that he could not hope to capture the bulk of the North Atlantic passenger business by building faster vessels. "Comfort—even luxury—will win the hearts of those who cross frequently," he is quoted as having said. Then he added, "It hardly needs to be said that first class will not suffice; steerage and cargo space are nearly as important and will cost far less."

Despite his disclaimer of the importance of speed, Ismay had a talk with chief engineer Joseph Bell while the steerage passengers were boarding the *Titanic* at Queenstown, Ireland. Although Ismay later denied it under oath, they seem to have agreed upon "a full speed run." There was no possibility of crossing in record time, but it might be possible to shave a few hours off the fastest time of the White Star's *Olympic*. Questioned by a *New York Times* reporter, Ismay went to great pains to stress that the *Titanic* "at no time during her voyage had been at full speed." If he was telling the truth, the shortage of coal at Southampton may have been so acute that some of the liner's immense boilers could not be fired on her maiden voyage.

Ismay's account of the way in which an ice warning was treated was even more nebulous than his testimony about speed. Wireless operator Jack Phillips received a brief message from the *Baltic* and sent it to Captain Smith. Shortly afterward the captain handed the warning to Ismay. Instead of returning it to Smith, who normally would have posted it in the officers' chart room, the executive "rather believed that he might have stuffed the *Baltic* message in his pocket." He said that he "seemed to remember" having later surmised that "Smith, who had many things on his mind, may have forgotten that ice lay somewhere ahead and we were likely to reach it during the night."

When ice was encountered hours earlier than expected, it was not in the form of relatively thin floating chunks that seamen accustomed to the North Atlantic took casually. There was a noticeable thud when the liner's side hit an iceberg. Startled in his cabin by the change in the rhythm of the ship, Ismay guessed the *Titanic* "may have lost a blade off a screw [propeller]."

Several survivors thought they saw Ismay helping women and children into lifeboats, but only a few were specific about his actions. T. D. M. Cardeza of Philadelphia, reported the *Times,* said, "Mr. Ismay had been persuaded to enter one of the lifeboats by the women who had already embarked in it." A story circulated that the Englishman boarded lifeboat number one and later "liberally rewarded the crew of this boat and had them photographed." This proved to be untrue.

Steward Edward B. Brown insisted that he saw Ismay helping to load Collapsible C, one of the Englehardts, the last lifeboat to leave the ship after being properly lowered. Ismay was in this boat when it was picked up by the *Carpathia* about five hours after the *Titanic* sank. Precisely how and why he got into it, wearing a suit and overcoat over his pajamas, became a hotly discussed matter.

During British hearings about the disaster, he was questioned about his reason for trying to save his life when hundreds of other persons—many of whom were women—were left behind to die. "I entered the boat," he explained, "because there was room in it.

She was being lowered away. I felt that the ship was going down and I got in the boat."

An officer of the rescue vessel *Carpathia* believed that Englehardt C was the ninth or tenth lifeboat to be picked up. "When he came aboard, soon after 6:00 A.M., I didn't know who Mr. Ismay was," he told a reporter. "I heard him demanding food, however, and saw a steward lead him to the dining room." About half an hour later, he was seen going into the cabin of the ship's surgeon. Dr. Frank McGee then personally placed a Do Not Enter notice on the door. A woman passenger on the *Carpathia* described Ismay as "being quite beside himself" when he climbed aboard. It was her belief that "on most of the voyage to New York he was being quieted by opiates on order of the ship's doctor."

Since many survivors were permitted to send messages to the Marconi cabin of the *Carpathia* for transmission to the mainland, Ismay dispatched to the Ritz Hotel a request for one of its best rooms. Yet Capt. Arthur H. Rostron of the rescue ship had to persuade Ismay to notify the New York office of the White Star Line about the loss of *Titanic*. After initially hesitating, Ismay directed a message to Phillip A. S. Franklin, U.S. vice president of the line: "Deeply regret to advise you Titanic sank this morning after collision with an iceberg, resulting in serious loss of life. Full particulars later. YAMSI."

The enigmatic signature, believed to be known only to top executives of the shipping companies of which he was in charge, served as Ismay's not-so-secret private designation. Hours later his backward-spelled surname ended another Marconi wireless in which he gave orders that the White Star liner *Cedric* should remain at New York until the arrival of the *Carpathia*. He did not say so in his brief instructions, but this arrangement would permit him to send surviving members of the *Titanic*'s crew to England immediately. J. Pierpont Morgan would appreciate this prompt action concerning these men, he was sure. Under the regulations of the IMM, the pay of crew members had stopped when the liner sank. Since an engineer, fireman, or steward might tell this to the press upon reaching New York, it was important that the surviving members of the crew be put aboard the *Cedric* and quickly returned to England.

According to the *Times,* in addition to Ismay, the Ritz provided rooms for "the Countess of Rothes, Lord and Lady Duff Gordon, T. D. M. Cardeza, Mrs. J. M. Cardeza, Miss L. P. Smith, Mrs.

PARTIAL LIST OF THE SAVED.

Includes Bruce Ismay, Mrs. Widener, Mrs. H. B. Harris, and an Incomplete name, suggesting Mrs. Astor's.

Special to The New York Times.

CAPE RACE, N. F., Tuesday, April 16.—Following is a partial list of survivors among the first-class passengers of the Titanic, received by the Marconi wireless station this morning from the Carpathia, via the steapship Olympic:

Mrs. JACOB P. ——— and maid.
Mr. HARRY ANDERSON.
Mrs. ED. W. APPLETON.
Mrs. ROSE ABBOTT.
Miss G. M. BURNS.
Miss D. D. CASSEBERE.
Mrs. WM. M. CLARKE.
Mrs. B. CHIBINACE.
Miss E. G. CROSSBIE.
Miss H. ROSEBIE.·
Miss JEAN HIPACK.
Mrs. HY. B. HARRIS.
Mrs. ALEX. HALVERSON.
Miss MARGARET BAYS.
Mr. BRUCE ISMAY.
Mr. and Mrs. ED. KIMBERLEY.
Mr. F. A. KENNYMAN.
Miss EMILE KENCHEN.
Miss G. F. LONGLEY.
Mrs. A. F. LEADER.
Miss BERTHA LAVORY.
Mrs. ERNEST LIVES.
Miss MARY CLINES.
Mrs. SINGRID LINDSTROM.
Mr. GUSTAVE J. LESNEUR.
Miss GIORGETTA A. MADILL.
Mme. MELICARD.
Mrs. TUCKER and maid.
Mrs. J. B. THAYER.
Mr. J. B. THAYER, Jr.
Mr. HENRY WOOLMER.
Miss ANNA WARD.
Mr. RICHARD M. WILLIAMS.
Mrs. F. M. WARNER.
Miss HELEN A. WILSON.
Miss WILLARD.
Miss MARY WICKS.
Mrs. GEO. D. WIDENER and maid.
Mrs. J. STEWART WHITE.
Miss MARIE YOUNG.
Mrs. THOMAS POTTER, Jr.
Mrs. EDNA S. ROBERTS.
Countess of ROTHES.

Mr. C. ROLMANE.
Mrs. SUSAN P. ROGERSON. (Probably Ryerson).
Miss EMILY P. ROGERSON.
Mrs. ARTHUR ROGERSON.
Master ALLISON and nurse.
Miss K. T. ANDREWS.
Miss NINETTE PANHART.
Miss E. W. ALLEN.
Mr. and Mrs. D. BISHOP.
Mr. H. BLANK.
Miss A. BASSINA.
Mrs. JAMES BAXTER.
Mr. GEORGE A. BATT···
Miss C. BONNELL.
Mrs. J. M. BROWN.
Miss G. C. BOWEN.
Mr. and Mrs. R. L. BECK···
Miss RUTH TAUSSIG.
Miss ELLA THOR.
Mr. and Mrs. E. Z. TAYLOR.
GILBERT M. TUCKER.
Mr. J. B. THAYER.
Mr. JOHN B. ROGERSON.
Mrs. M. ROTHSCHILD.
Miss MADELEINE NEWELL.
Mrs. MARJORIE NEWELL.
HELEN W. NEWSOM.
Mr. FIENNAD OMOND.
Mr. E. C. OSTBY.
Miss HELEN R. OSTBY.
Mrs. MAMAM J. RENAGO.
Mlle. OLIVIA.
Mrs. D. W. MERVIN.
Mr. PHILIP EMOCK.
Mr. JAMES GOOGHT.
Mrs. RUBERTA MAIMY.
Mr. PIERRE MARECHAL.
Mr. W. E. MINEHAN.
Miss APPIE RANELT.
Major ARTUR PEUCHEN.
Mrs. KARL H. BEHR.
Miss DESSETTE.

Mrs. WILLIAM BUCKNELL.
Mrs. O. H. BARKWORTH.
Mrs. H. B. STEFFASON.
Mrs. ELSIE BOWERMAN.

The Marconi station reports that it missed the word after " Mrs. Jacob P." In a list received by the Associated Press this morning this name appeared well down, but in THE TIMES list it is first, suggesting that the name of Mrs. John Jacob Astor is intended. This supposition is strengthened by the fact that, except for Mrs. H. J. Allison, Mrs. Astor is the only lady in the " A " column of the ship's passenger list attended by a maid.

NAMES PICKED UP AT BOSTON.

BOSTON, April 15.—Among the names of survivors of the Titanic picked up by wireless from the steamer Carpathia here to-night were the following:

Mr. and Mrs. L. HENRY.
Mrs. W. A. HOOPER.
Mr. MILE.
Mr. J. FLYNN.
Miss ALICE FORTUNE.
Mrs. ROBERT DOUGLAS.
Miss HILDA SLAYTER.
Mrs. P. SMITH.
Mrs. BRAHAM.
Miss LUCILLE CARTER.
Mr. WILLIAM CARTER.
Miss CUMMINGS.
Mrs. FLORENCE MARE.
Miss ALICE PHILLIPS.
Mrs. PAULA MUNGE.
Mrs. JANE ———
Miss PHYLLIS O. ———
HOWARD B. CASE.
Miss MINEHAN.
Miss BERTHA ———

The first published list of survivors from Titanic*'s first class included Ismay's name, fifteenth from the top in the first column. It was his standard practice to be on the maiden voyage of each new ship in the White Star Line. Ismay made notes constantly of improvements and enhancements that could be incorporated on the next ship to be built. His name among the* Titanic*'s survivors, however, only raised eyebrows and placed a shadow over his reputation.*

George D. Widener, Mrs. Kinslop, M. Simenonios, and Mrs. Robert Clark." At the Belmont Hotel, newspaper readers were informed, were: "Mr. and Miss Compton, Mrs. Appleton and Mrs. Brown, the last two named being sisters of Magistrate Cornell's wife, Mrs. Mark Fortune." Most other first-class passengers and some who traveled second class went to less prominent hotels;

Following his appearance before the Senate subcommittee investigating the sinking of the Titanic, *Ismay returned to England and found that he had been judged a coward by the news media on both sides of the Atlantic.*

most members of the crew were immediately transshipped to England; and steerage passengers who did not have relatives in New York were herded into a makeshift temporary shelter.

Within hours after having reached the Ritz, Ismay decided that it would be wise to refuse to give interviews, as the U.S. Senate planned to hold an inquiry at once. A statement that he released to the *Times* included a pledge: "I heartily welcome an exhaustive inquiry, and any aid that I or my associates or navigators can render is at the service of the public and the Governments of the United States and Great Britain."

He knew he was being bitterly assailed for having taken to the Englehardt boat when many women and even more men were still on the sinking liner. Newspapers were castigating him so strongly that the British consul in New York sent a message to Sir Edward Grey, the foreign secretary, in London, in which he said:

> During this sad times, and especially during the first two days, a great deal of pain was caused to the public by the improper use of wireless by unauthorized amateurs. The American press has been perfectly hysterical over the disaster, and has pub-

lished wild and untrue statements without taking any trouble
to justify them. The particular butt has been Mr. Bruce Ismay,
whose conduct has been most unjustly criticised.

Sen. William A. Smith of Michigan, a member of the Senate
Committee on Commerce, led in the creation of a subcommittee
charged with inquiring into the disaster. The U.S. investigation
began on April 19 with Ismay the first witness to be questioned.
Yes, he said in response to an inquiry by Smith, he was the sole
representative of the White Star Line aboard the doomed vessel. It
was his custom to sail on the maiden voyages of his ships "in order
to discover what improvements could be made." In the vernacular
of the sea, he spoke of the *Titanic*'s speed in terms of revolutions
of her propeller rather than in knots or miles per hour. She was
capable of attaining eighty revolutions per minute, he said, "but
did not reach seventy-five until the third day and thereafter never
exceeded that speed."

A committee member asked if it were true that he had planned
to drive the liner forward at top speed in order to reach New York
half a day ahead of schedule. "That was my intention when we
stopped at Queenstown," he admitted. "On both Monday and
Tuesday, however, we failed to have the fine weather we anticipated, so five of the vessel's single-ended boilers were not fired."

During the subsequent British inquiry, Ismay answered nearly
850 questions. Many of them dealt with the widespread public
belief that he survived only because he exerted his power as an
executive of the line that owned and operated the *Titanic*. He stubbornly insisted that he had assisted numerous women into
lifeboats, although he did not know their names. He admitted that
early on the morning of April 15 he had boarded the last lifeboat
to leave "except one which later washed into the sea, upside
down." At the time he stepped from the sinking ship, he said over
and over, no other passengers were near it. "I am absolutely positive that no woman was in sight," he said.

Members of the British commission refused to censure Ismay,
but to most eyes its action seemed to be a whitewash. Ismay's conduct aboard the *Titanic* was assailed so furiously and so constantly
that he went into seclusion and for the rest of his life seldom ventured into public places.

In retrospect it appears true that Ismay deliberately took the
steps necessary to save his own life. It is also apparently true that

dozens of male passengers and crew members took to the lifeboats long before Ismay boarded Englehardt C. Had he been in the first lifeboat to pull away from the sinking liner, his conduct would have been inexcusable. Since he stayed on deck almost to the end before climbing into a lifeboat that was only half-filled, Ismay seems to have been made the scapegoat for all the mistakes that were made on that night of horror.

17

J. PIERPONT MORGAN

TAPESTRIES VERSUS THE TITANIC

IT'S COMMON knowledge that you will make the maiden voyage of the *Titanic*. I suppose that means you'll be embarking at Cherbourg?"

Briefly impaling his business acquaintance with his gimlet eyes, J. Pierpont Morgan turned his head without a word. Throughout the financial circles of the Western world the crusty seventy-year-old known as "the banker's banker" was noted for his taciturn ways. He refused to give interviews, rarely sat for a photographer, seldom answered a question, and preferred his own company to that of anyone else. Many times, he invited guests to his New York brownstone residence for a social evening, then withdrew into an alcove and sat there silently or played solitaire for the better part of an hour.

Perhaps because he was presently in the smoking room of a Paris hotel, perhaps because through the window he could glimpse row after row of tulips in glorious bloom, he chewed his big black cigar briefly, then turned to his visitor.

"Gossip is right, this time," he conceded. "I wouldn't miss that trip for a million dollars. But I will board at Southampton in order to make the entire voyage. Now to business, if you please."

For half an hour the French antiquities dealer who had come to Morgan's hotel at his request drew sketches and offered oral descriptions of a set of medieval tapestries belonging to an impoverished nobleman who wished to remain anonymous. These rare treasures depicted events of the Third Crusade to the Holy Land, he assured the American. They presently were in a castle little more than an hour away from Chartres. A prospective purchaser would be required to sign an agreement never to divulge the name of the

J. Pierpont Morgan's shipping combine, the International Mercantile Marine (IMM), acquired the White Star Line in 1902. He attended the launching of the Titanic *in 1911 and inspected the area in which a special cabin was to be built for his exclusive use. In 1912 Morgan had planned to be aboard for the ship's maiden voyage, but other business prevented him from doing so.*

seller. These treasures were worthy of a place in a renowned museum, he stressed before suggesting, "If you succeed in acquiring these works of art I believe you will wish to exhibit them—at least briefly."

Morgan's interest in the *Titanic* stemmed from the fact that his International Mercantile Marine holding company had acquired the White Star Line. Although he had reserved a suite at a cost of what would seem a fortune to an ordinary working man, he pushed all thought of the ocean liner aside at the mention of the medieval tapestries.

The financier had no training in art, but after his semiretirement he became interested—"nearly obsessed," according to some subordinates—with costly things of beauty. To every dealer with whom he talked, Morgan made it clear that he was interested in nothing but the best, with price being a minor consideration. As a result, by 1912 he had amassed collections that the experts of the day estimated to be worth at least fifty million dollars. Morgan's marble library was packed with one-of-a-kind manuscripts, illuminations, and incunabula (books printed before 1501). Having made plans to bequeath many of his rare minia-

White Star Line

PALATIAL ROYAL MAIL STEAMERS
"OLYMPIC," 45,324 tons
AND
"TITANIC" 45,000 tons,
are the Largest Vessels in the World
(Fitted with Marconi Wireless Apparatus.)
"OLYMPIC" sails from Southampton and Cher-
bourg to New York regularly.
"TITANIC" sails from Southampton
and Cherbourg on first voyage to
New York April 10, 1912

White Star Line

Few people were as anxious for the success of the new line of White Star luxury liners as Morgan. His disappointment was only compounded when the chairman of the Senate subcommittee investigating the disaster, William Alden Smith, took a special interest in Morgan's relationship to the ship and suspected negligence or malfeasance which in some way would be attributable to Morgan himself.

tures, ivories, woodcarvings, and enamels to New York's Metropolitan Museum of Art, he had spent the summer in Europe seeking to acquire statuary, paintings, and bronzes. Until he had been informed by a dealer with whom he had done a great deal of business, he had no idea that a unique set of medieval tapestries would soon be on the market.

"You must make arrangements for me to have a private viewing," Morgan demanded.

"That will be difficult," the dealer replied, "but perhaps it can be done. You must be patient."

Morgan waited impatiently for a week before notifying the dealer that he must see the collection soon or not at all. Then just as he was preparing to leave for England, he received word that the arrangements had been made and he could view the tapestries and make an offer for them.

The centerpiece of the elegant liner's decor was the grand staircase above. Above it was an ornate, white-enameled, wrought-iron skylight on A Deck. It descended through four decks to the entrance to the first-class dining room on D Deck, incorporating a William-and-Mary style and a Louis XIV balustrade.

MORGAN WAS the son of an international banker who became a partner of George Peabody and amassed a fortune by buying and selling stage coaches, hotels, and insurance companies. J. P. later formed an alliance with the Drexels of Philadelphia. He engaged in a furious contest with Jay Gould and Jim Fisk over control of the Albany and Susquehanna Railroad, then broke Jay Cooke's monopoly in the refunding of federal governmental operations.

At age forty-six, with his star rising rapidly, Morgan's British connections enabled him to sell abroad huge blocks of stock in the New York Central Railroad, which was controlled by William H. Vanderbilt. This coup seems to have led him to concentrate almost exclusively upon the transportation industry for a decade during

Morgan's all-encompassing business interests gave him a high profile in the early twentieth century prior to World War I. One cartoonist depicted him as holding the world in his hands.

which he bought and sold railroads like others traded horses. He was not satisfied to hold interests in the Erie Railway, the Philadelphia and Reading, the Southern Pacific, and the Northern Pacific. Forming a business alliance with James H. Hill, he gained a powerful voice in the operation of the Pennsylvania Railroad and the Northern Pacific.

In 1895 Morgan's firm sold all of a sixty-two million dollar government bond issue, ending a gold shortage in the U.S. Treasury. During the Panic of 1907, Morgan lent money to banks to keep them from closing. After having financed the Federal Steel Company, the National Tube Company, and the American Bridge Company, he persuaded Andrew Carnegie and William H. Vanderbilt to cooperate with him in the organization of the United States Steel Corporation. Nearly a century passed before a larger corporate merger was effected.

His passionate interest in transportation influenced him to build the yacht *Columbia,* with which he defeated Sir Thomas Lipton's *Shamrock* in a contest for the coveted Americas Cup. Morgan then turned more attention to the sea, organizing the

International Mercantile Marine in 1902. With the new holding company, he set out to acquire enough steamship lines to gain a monopoly in the lucrative North Atlantic trade. It was this venture that brought him control of the *Titanic* and her two monstrous sister ships, the *Olympic* and the *Britannic*.

ARRIVING AT his French destination ready to make an offer if the tapestries were as represented, Morgan experienced another delay of several days. While waiting, he sent a cancellation message to Southampton saying that urgent business prevented him from boarding the *Titanic* for her voyage to New York.

Reticent by nature, the man who rarely delivered a speech and who wrote no articles or books said nothing about the way fate prevented him from sailing on the doomed liner. Less than a year later, however, on March 31, 1913, Morgan died in Rome, Italy.

18

VERY EARLY MONDAY

WOMEN AND CHILDREN FIRST

ABOUT HALF an hour after the collision, Elizabeth W. Shutes's concern had turned to worry. She knew that many people from first class had gathered on deck shortly after midnight, and she took seriously her responsibility as governess of Margaret Graham. Although there were no loud noises and few signs of commotion, she decided that something of importance must have drawn the passengers from their cozy quarters at such an hour.

Stepping from the Grahams' cabin, Shutes called out to a member of the crew as he rushed by. Striding rapidly down the passageway, he paused a moment for her to catch up with him. She wanted to know if the liner was experiencing trouble, and he chuckled and tossed her a quick "Of course not!" before continuing on his way. Shutes turned and reentered the cabin still feeling worried. Minutes later a room steward arrived to inform her that the captain had ordered everyone in first class to go on deck immediately.

Margaret Graham, who corroborated the account given by her governess, estimated that they had been on deck about twenty minutes when "suddenly a very bright white light shot into the air." Although she did not know it at the time, this was a rocket to notify nearby vessels that the ship was in distress.

Having reached the decision to resort to the lifeboats, the captain appointed Second Officer Lightoller to supervise the entire operation. "Take care to see that two crewmen are in each boat," Smith ordered. Both men knew that their vessel carried two cutters rated at 40 passengers, fourteen standard thirty-foot lifeboats designed to hold 65 people comfortably, and four Englehardts holding 47 each. Collectively, the twenty boats should accommodate 1,178 adults. Additional emergency gear later enumerated by the *New York Times* consisted of 3,455 life preservers and 48 life buoys. Lightoller instructed the crewmen to make sure that all who entered the boats had donned life jackets.

Around 12:30 A.M. Lightoller shouted to the passengers gathered near lifeboat number seven, "Women and children first!" The passengers correctly interpreted this as an order, not a suggestion. Similar instructions were given throughout the ship. Lookout Archie Jewell and his fellow crew members working at the starboard side of the ship had trouble manipulating the immense davits that lowered the boats. By about 12:45, however, number seven had come off the boat deck and was swinging level with A Deck. Rated to hold 65 adults but large enough to accommodate 70 without serious crowding, number seven swung to the water far below with only 27 people aboard. Despite Lightoller's order concerning priorities, French aviator Pierre Marechal and Philadelphia banker James R. McGough were among those in the less-than-half-filled boat when its occupants rowed away from the doomed liner. During the U.S. Senate inquiry, Mrs. Helen Bishop of Dowagiac, Michigan, said that when the boat was lowered it held just 8 women. Jewell and 2 other members of the crew plus 7 male passengers were also aboard, she testified.

Lifeboat number five was being loaded on the same side. When all women close at hand had crawled into the boat, Third Officer H. J. Pitman signaled for nearby men to enter it. Although she did not know him then, from a published photograph later, Marguerite Frolicher identified J. Bruce Ismay as one of the men supervising the loading. Sailors started lowering this lifeboat into the water about ten minutes after number seven, although even with the men aboard it was far from full. Messrs. Henry W. and T. G. Fruenthal noticed that there was ample space left, so both of them jumped from the deck. One landed without mishap, but his brother fell on Mrs. Annie Stengel and knocked her unconscious.

With bedlam reigning across the boat deck, some observers later said they thought that the first boat to be put to use was number six on the port side of the liner. A majority of survivors, however, said that it was the third lifeboat to be put into service. Whatever the sequence, Lightoller supervised this one himself, and the only men aboard were quartermaster Robert Hitchens and lookout Fred Fleet.

It is possible that Lightoller and other supervisors of the lifeboats initially believed that these wooden craft would snap in

While Second Officer Charles H. Lightoller was charged with the responsibility of getting the passengers into the lifeboats, he assigned himself to the port boats and strictly enforced the order regarding women and children first. First Officer William Murdoch (left) directed the starboard side operations and was much more lenient in allowing men into the boats, which may be why he completed his work nearly half an hour earlier than did Lightoller.

two if fully loaded. Whether that was so or not, he signaled for number six to drop downward when it held Mrs. J. J. "Maggie" Brown and about two dozen other women plus Fleet and Hitchens.

As boat number six was being lowered, one of the women called up to Lightoller, "We've only one seaman in the boat!" There were no crewmen near the second officer, and so he called out to the crowd of people around him, "Any seamen there?" Maj. Arthur Godfrey Peuchen stepped forward and said that he was a yachtsman. "Well, if you're seaman enough to get out on that fall," Lightoller replied, "you can go." Peuchen climbed onto the railing and grasped the front line by which the lifeboat was being lowered and climbed down into the lifeboat. He later told friends that under those circumstances he could not agonize over having left in his stateroom a stack of bonds and other securities. "I was fortunate, indeed, barely to escape with my life," he mused.

Having started from amidship, First Officer William M. Murdoch and his detail worked their way aft. With numbers seven and five on the water, they turned to number three. Since the *Titanic*'s starboard list had become more pronounced by this time, it was difficult to prevent a boat from banging against the liner's side as it was lowered. Having this additional reason to hurry, sailors dropped number three when it was about half full. After twenty or

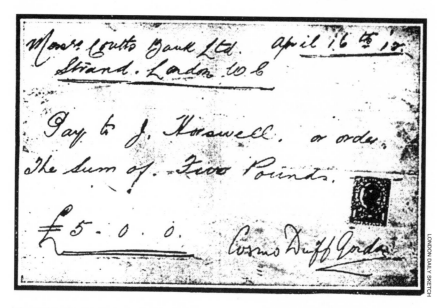

Lord Duff Gordon handed promissory notes like the one above to each of the crew members in his lifeboat. To some observers he was bribing them not to pick up any other possible survivors, but he claimed that he was only thanking them with money so they could purchase the necessities they needed for their next berthing—those items which they had lost with the Titanic.

more women and children had entered it, no more were immediately at hand. Murdoch nodded, and between ten and fifteen crew members jumped into the boat. One of its occupants, Mrs. Charles M. Hays, was nearly hysterical as she waved frantically in the direction of her husband who was leaning over the rail of the liner.

Fourth Officer Joseph G. Boxhall was not involved in loading the boats. He was busy pulling out socket signals and the mortars from which they were fired. Just before 1:00 A.M. he sent a distress signal of this sort more than six hundred feet into the air. Upon reaching the top of its trajectory, it exploded and a dozen white stars drifted downward. After having fired at least nine or ten such rockets, he had exhausted his supply when the last went off about 1:30.

Now working more smoothly on both sides of the stricken liner, members of the crew launched lifeboats numbers nine and ten simultaneously. When number nine was about two-thirds full, an unidentified woman "somewhat advanced in years" balked and refused to enter it. Mrs. Jacques Futrelle, who had been led to the spot by her husband, also resisted efforts to get her into the boat, but her husband got behind her and pushed her to make sure that she did not remain on deck. Although an estimated sixty adults were aboard, the sturdy boat did not even bend under its load.

Now severely hampered by the listing of the *Titanic,* men loading number ten struggled manfully and managed to get more than forty women into it. Any man who seemed to be trying to enter the boat was waved aside by Sixth Officer James Moody. He had no way of knowing it, but the vessel already had two men aboard. They were unidentified stowaways who had managed to crawl into the vessel, had hidden under canvas, and emerged only after the ship had been on the water for some time.

Before they began the laborious job of lowering the lifeboats, Smith, Murdoch, Lightoller, and the other officers knew that there were not enough lifeboats for the passengers and crew. Her lifeboats had been put aboard in accordance with British regulations adopted in 1894, when the largest liner afloat was the *Lucania,* rated at just less than 13 tons. Board of Trade regulations required the 45,000-ton *Titanic* to carry enough lifeboats and/or life rafts to hold 962 people. Although the ship exceeded these regulations by providing boats for nearly 1,200 persons, an estimated 2,200 passengers and crew were aboard. When the order stipulating women and children first was initially given, the ship's officers knew that after every lifeboat was filled to capacity or beyond, about 1,000 people—presumably men—would go down with the doomed liner.

Three days after the disaster, the *Times* revealed that there were not enough lifeboats on the *Titanic* for everyone. Supervising Inspector General George Uhler, head of the U.S. Steamboat Inspection Service, was quoted as having explained that operators of ocean liners did not pretend to carry "enough lifeboats to save the lives of all if a vessel goes down." Since the *Titanic* was registered in Great Britain as a Royal Mail Steamer, Americans were not entitled to inspect her. "Figuring the Titanic as of 46,000 tons," said Uhler, "under the United States law she would have to have had accommodations for 2,412 persons."

In a later edition, an editorial in the *Times* castigated the owners and operators of the liner: "It seems an assured fact that if the Titanic had carried enough lifeboats to hold all its human cargo there would have been no loss of life. Lifeboats have been regarded,

on these splendid modern ships, as mere concessions to the preju-
dices of the traveling public. There will be a spontaneous call now
for more lifeboats, a sufficient number for any emergency, on all
passenger ships, even if some of the space given over to purposes of
comfort and luxury must be sacrificed to make room for them."

Around 1:10 A.M., on the port side, lifeboat number eight was
launched, with Mrs. Ida Straus relinquishing her place when she
found that her husband would not be permitted to go with her. Testimony at the British inquiry after the disaster fixed the number of
boat eight's occupants at thirty-eight. Of these, the only men aboard
were the sailor who was in charge, two stewards, and a cook.

A few minutes later on the starboard side, boat number eleven
had been packed with about seventy people before others were
barred from entering it. A young society matron, Mrs. Emma Schu-
bert, afterward said that there were some men aboard. "They persisted in smoking after having been asked to desist," she recalled.

Lifeboats numbers twelve and thirteen, on opposite sides of
the liner, are believed to have hit the water at about 1:25 A.M. A
considerable number of second class and steerage men seem to
have attempted to get into number twelve, but they were driven off
by Lightoller and his men. As a result, the boat had only forty-two
aboard when some of its passengers began rowing away from the
liner. Only around twenty-one people—chiefly women and children from steerage—had piled into number thirteen when the
davits began to creak as it started its descent.

About this time, reported some survivors, many of the ship's
officers pulled out their revolvers and brandished them at "half-
crazed males who tried to rush some of the boats." Numerous
accounts of the last half hour of the *Titanic* include assertions that
gunshots were heard at more than one point. Whether or not these
memories are accurate, it is impossible to determine. The rumor
that one of the shots was self-inflicted by Captain Smith appears
to have been without foundation. All who knew him were unani-
mous in saying that he was no man to commit suicide, and a handful of witnesses were reasonably sure they saw him on the bridge
as the liner began its plunge into the depths.

An unidentified survivor was positive that when lifeboat number
fourteen was lowered, it held "a cur in human form." An utterly
despicable man, according to this account, raced through an open
door into a deserted stateroom, donned a skirt, hat, and a heavy
veil. So disguised, he reputedly "filched a place in the lifeboat and
thereby saved his skin but in doing so gave up his good name."

The boat known as Collapsible B had entered the water capsized. Second Officer Lightoller managed to get thirty men to balance themselves on its keel and eventually caught up with the other boats. In the early morning light it tied up with a knot of other lifeboats, and the men cautiously moved into the other boats.

On the port side number sixteen was the aftermost standard lifeboat. By now seamen were trying to make sure that there were fewer empty spaces in the boats, so this one saved the lives of about fifty passengers and six members of the crew. Elizabeth Leather and Violet Jessup both took turns at an oar.

Also on the port side, lifeboat number two may have been the last to be lowered at about 1:45 A.M. An emergency cutter rated for forty passengers, it probably carried twenty-one women and five men to safety. Lightoller was reported to have been more strict about women and children first than was Murdoch, who directed the starboard side operations. This factor may explain why Murdoch completed his work nearly half an hour earlier than did Lightoller on the opposite side of the liner.

Four Englehardt boats whose wooden bodies were topped by sides of folding canvas were the last to be launched. Seamen attempted to attach each of them, in turn, to the davits previously used to lower conventional lifeboats.

In charge of Englehardt C, Murdoch seems to have decided to save as many lives as possible. Testimony in England indicated that he packed seventy-one desperate persons into a craft rated for a maximum load of forty-seven. If that count were accurate, this comparatively small boat was the most heavily laden of all that left the *Titanic*. At least one American survivor, Col. Archibald Gracie, was positive that the number who pulled away in Englehardt C was greatly exaggerated by its occupants, among whom were J. Bruce Ismay and American businessman William E. Carter.

In charge of Englehardt D, Lightoller stood by his women-and-children-first rule. He reputedly had seamen stand close together in a semicircle with locked arms. One man who had managed to reach the site of the launch from his second-class quarters urged two small boys along the deck in front of him. When the circle was broken to permit the children to go to the boat, the man who was thought to be their father turned away to go down with the ship. He had appeared on the passenger list as "Mr. Hoffman, with Lolo and Louis." The orphan children were given shelter in New York after the rescue ship docked. Not until weeks later, when their mother saw published pictures of the children, were they identified as Michael and Edmond Navatril, later described as having been "kidnaped by their distraught father who was going through divorce proceedings."

Eyewitness testimony concerning Englehardt B was conflicting. Some persons were sure that as it was being prepared for use, a heavy wave tumbled over the down-pointed bow of the *Titanic* and washed the boat overboard. Others were equally positive that all efforts to get it ready failed, so it overturned and simply floated away when the liner vanished under it. Regardless of how it got into the water upside down, this boat functioning like a raft became a lifesaver to Gracie, Lightoller, and a number of others.

According to lists compiled by *Times* staff members and published on April 16, 866 women, children, and men were saved, but 1,254 persons were considered to be "probably drowned." As additional word came from the rescue ship *Carpathia*, these figures were revised several times daily. On April 17, readers were told that 1,595 persons died when the "unsinkable" liner went to the bottom. Two days later, a boxed tabulation reduced the number of the missing to 1,514. That is very close to the total arrived at from data that were compiled during decades of research.

Nowhere do class distinctions of the era show up more clearly than in the comparison of those who were saved with those who died. Approximately half of the first-class passengers died; the majority of the survivors were women and children. About 70 percent of the second-class travelers died despite the fact that scores of women and children in this category were saved. Crew members fared as poorly as steerage passengers; the death rate for both groups was a horrific 80 percent.

19

FOUR HOURS PLUS

THE CRUEL SEA

ALONG WITH eight or nine other fellows, I managed to get hold of the upturned [Englehardt B] boat," fireman Harry Senior said. "It must have been a little after 2:00 o'clock." For several minutes after he entered the subfreezing water he clung to a floating piece of debris. Had waves not washed the lifeboat from the liner, he would have remained in the water and would have frozen to death in another half hour, at most.

Later, while describing the horror, Senior refuted the report that Captain Smith had shot himself when he saw the hopelessness of the situation. "With the bow of the *Titanic* headed down and about to go completely under," the fireman reported, "Capt. Smith jumped from the promenade deck. He had an infant clutched tightly in his arms. They hit the water together."

According to Senior, the captain and the small child landed not far from Englehardt B. "It took him only a few strokes to reach the upturned life boat," he recalled. "At least a dozen hands reached out to take the little fellow from him and drag him to safety. After that, some of us dragged the captain from the water."

Senior's account concluded: "Capt. Smith had on a life buoy and a life preserver. He clung there a moment and then he slid off again and was soon out of my reach." Like dozens of other firsthand recollections, the fireman's story of the way in which his captain died was never corroborated by any other survivors. On the overturned lifeboat, most of the men who had scrambled upon it lay prone with exhaustion.

Soon after Smith had ordered the women and children into the *Titanic*'s lifeboats, a Philadelphia resident noticed one of the ship's eight musicians "walking in a great hurry." Since he carried a big instrument in his arms, he was presumed to be the popular cellist Percy Taylor. Not long afterward, Taylor and the rest of the musicians began to play. By the time Second Officer Lightoller took charge of loading the boats, the entire "orchestra," as it was called in White Star advertisements, had assembled and gone to work.

While at lifeboat number six, Lightoller wrote afterward, "I could hear the band playing cheery sort of music. I don't like jazz music as a rule, but I was glad to hear it that night. I think it helped us all." Many survivors testified, "To a man, the musicians stuck to their instruments to the very last. All eight of them went down with the ship."

A few days later Mrs. Vera Dick tried to describe her last hour on the liner and her first hour in a lifeboat to a *New York Times* reporter:

> After the ship had run into the iceberg not one of the passengers realized that there was the least danger. They just strolled about the decks and chatted about the ice field and the usual gossip of a steamship.
>
> No one seemed to realize the danger when the first two boats were loaded. That's why they had so many men in them.
>
> My husband and I tried to get others in our boat to be quiet so that we could hear the beautiful music that was coming from the *Titanic*. They played to the very end, and were rendering "Nearer, My God to Thee" when the rising water put an end to the strangest concert anyone ever attended.

ALTHOUGH NUMEROUS other passengers said they vividly remembered the hymn identified by Mrs. Dick, considerable evidence suggests that their imaginations were playing tricks upon them. Small wonder; in addition to music from the sinking ship, they heard multitudes of men and women gasping and trying to cry for help as they floundered in the icy water.

Second wireless operator Harold S. Bride, whose story was the first to be given to the public, was firm in his recollection that the final music of the band was "Autumn," and the majority of survivors attest to the accuracy of Bride's observations and memory. Since the song includes a line about perils of the sea, to band leader Wallace Hartley it could have been judged appropriate for his final music.

Debate over the melody that wafted from the liner as it went down was low key compared with the controversy concerning

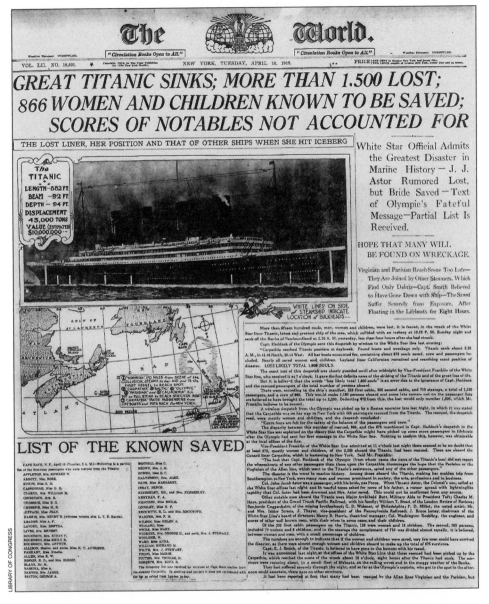

When the news finally spread that the Titanic had been lost at sea, hardly a newspaper on either side of the Atlantic failed to make it a front-page story.

precisely what happened to her during her last few minutes afloat. Of one thing Lightoller was positive: The ship lurched under him at the last, which caused him to fall into the water. Strangely, he did not go below the subfreezing surface; he landed on top of a funnel grating in spread-eagle style. From that temporary shelter he managed to reach the overturned Englehardt boat, from which he saw the *Titanic* disappear.

Perhaps because her bow had been pointed downward for some time, a majority of the more than seven hundred people in or on top of the water were sure that the ship went down in one piece. Relatively few survivors, one of whom was seventeen-year-old Jack Thayer, voiced a different description. According to him, the gigantic vessel broke in two, probably at a point between her third and fourth funnels. Thayer said that the bow sank immediately afterward, with the stern quickly following it into the depths. To the surprise of many who escaped death that dreadful morning, J. Bruce Ismay supported the account given by young Thayer.

Not having had the benefit of Ismay's expert testimony, a reporter for the *Times* told readers: "The bow went under first and then the huge bulk slowly settled until she stood nearly upright, with 15 feet showing out of water. There she hung, a fascinating but fearful spectacle, and then dropped slowly out of sight." It was this general description on which a majority of early artists relied when they sketched the final moments of the great liner.

Scores of persons in lifeboats—veteran sailors as well as landlubbers—were almost petrified with fear that they would be drawn into a vortex by the suction created by the sinking ship. Panic caused those who were at the oars of the lifeboats to row with frantic haste to put enough distance between themselves and the anticipated suction, which never came. It was this frenzy, some of them later confessed, that caused the occupants of some half-filled boats to disregard cries for help from the drowning.

Numerous survivors testified that they heard explosions just before the liner sank, but they disagreed about the number of noises the foundering vessel gave out. Groping for a way to account for these sounds, some longtime seamen surmised that the ship's enormous boilers broke loose and ripped forward when the bow reached a critical angle.

Practically all the survivors agreed concerning one somewhat puzzling aspect of the *Titanic*'s last half hour. She was equipped with thousands of electric lights that gave the vessel a stunning appearance when seen from a distance on a clear night. Most of these lights were glowing brightly when the first lifeboat pulled away from the liner. The occupants of several lifeboats were positive that the lights continued to burn after water inside the vessel had crept past them. According to them, the *Titanic* was dark only a few seconds before she disappeared. Logically, the electrical circuits would have shorted out when the water surged over several of her decks, but the survivors insist that this did not take place.

In his account of the sinking, Lawrence Beesley claimed:

> As we gazed awe-struck, she tilted slowly up, revolving apparently about a center of gravity just astern of amidships, until she attained a vertically upright position; and there she remained—motionless! As she swung up, her lights, which had shone without a flicker all night, went out suddenly, came on again for a single flash, then went out altogether. And as they did so, there came a noise which many people, wrongly I think, have described as an explosion; it has always seemed to me that it was nothing but the engines and machinery coming loose from their bolts and bearings, and falling through the compartments, smashing everything in their way. It was partly a roar, partly a groan, partly a rattle, and partly a smash, and it was not a sudden roar as an explosion would be: it went on successively for some seconds, possibly fifteen to twenty. . . .
>
> No phenomenon like that pictured in some American and English papers occurred—that of the ship breaking in two, and the two ends being raised above the surface. When the noise was over the *Titanic* was still upright like a column: we could see her now only as the stern and some 150 feet of her stood outlined against the star-specked sky, and in this position she continued for some minutes—I think as much as five minutes, but it may have been less.

First-class passengers Dickinson and Helen Bishop concurred with Beesley's description. They told a *Times* reporter that after the *Titanic* assumed a perpendicular position "it seemed to us that it stood upright in the water for four full minutes." Mrs. Edgar Meyer, closely related to the family whose members controlled New York's Saks and Company, did not remember the position of the *Titanic* when her lifeboat was still fairly near it, but she said that she heard "a noise that seemed as though it might have come from a dozen locomotives, all blowing off steam at once."

By the time the liner disappeared, some of the survivors believed that they were at least a mile away from the point at which the ship sank. Captain Smith, who clearly knew better, failed to take into account the fact that each oar on a lifeboat demanded the muscles and skill of two persons, not one. Smith's order that two crewmen should be put into each lifeboat, theoretically carrying no one but women and children, meant that in most of the boats the women would have to help man the oars.

Custom, if not Board of Trade regulations, stipulated that every lifeboat should be equipped with a supply of bread and water. Possibly it was considered unnecessary, as this precaution was not taken. An unidentified ship's baker reportedly threw loaves of bread to the people in one or two boats; in the rest, there was neither bread nor water. As a result, more than seven hundred men, women, and children found themselves on the open sea in hard-to-manage boats with no light visible except the stars. Their emotions ran the full gamut of human experience as they tried to row the heavy boats with no idea of the direction in which they were slowly moving.

Some sobbed and others moaned as they thought of loved ones and acquaintances who had gone down with the ship. By the time she reached New York and solid ground, Mrs. Renee Harris was hysterical. According to the *Times,* when met by a party of friends, "She fell into the arms of her brother-in-law, crying: 'My God! Poor Harry! He wanted to get into the lifeboats, but he stepped back." Mrs. Helen Candee of Washington told the reporter of Ida Straus's refusal to abandon her husband, Isidor.

Mrs. Martha Stephenson of Haverford, Pennsylvania, described her last glimpse of John B. Thayer, vice president of the Pennsylvania Railroad: "Along with his adolescent son and a score of other males," she said, "Thayer refused to enter a lifeboat and chose to take his chances on a crude raft. He and others had scarcely jumped to the raft when a huge wave hit it, splitting it in two parts. Mr. Thayer, Sr., was thrown into the water and disappeared. His son managed to scramble back on the raft, and was rescued by one of the lifeboats."

A special dispatch to the *Times* noted that Washington A. Roebling II, nephew of the engineer who was in charge of constructing the Brooklyn Bridge, was among those whose end was unknown. Described as having been "an enthusiastic autoist who recently

LIBRARY OF CONGRESS

As the Titanic *survivors converged on the* Carpathia, *some boarded by rope ladders, children were hoisted up in mail sacks, and some of the women were lifted aboard in slings.*

took part in races at Savannah, Ga.," the dead man was just thirty-one years old. He boarded the *Titanic* after having "toured Italy, France, and other countries in an auto."

Nothing was known about the last hours of Wyckoff Vanderhoef, secretary of the Williamsburg Fire Insurance Company. Neither did any survivor have firsthand knowledge about Emil Brandeis, who had paid about $4,350 for what he expected to be a splendid crossing. Despite the fact that Clarence Moore was well known to many in first class, as he was a member of the New York Yacht Club and the Travelers' Club of Paris, no one knew whether he jumped into the sea or remained aboard the sinking *Titanic.* Jacques Futrelle, a journalist and author, refused to take a place in a lifeboat. At the Belmont Hotel his wife told a reporter that she begged him to get into a boat but he shook his head and walked away.

Two days after the disaster, the *Times* put into print what great numbers of Americans were thinking and saying. In a "TRIBUTE

The lack of sufficient lifeboats for all of Titanic's *passengers seemed to be the greatest and most obvious oversight in modern shipbuilding.*

LIFEBOATS FOR ALL NOT ORDERED BY LAW

Apparent Security of Modern Liners Kept Out-of-Date Requirements in Force.

SPACE FOR BOATS LIMITED

Faith in the Bulkheads Had Minimized the Necessity for Better Life-Saving Appliances.

NEW YORK TIMES

TO TITANIC DEAD," men who sacrificed their lives for women were lauded as having been "True Americans." In many cities editors and artists vied with one another in praising the men who deliberately let half-filled lifeboats depart without them.

Many of the women and children who were in the lifeboats had been reluctant to leave the ship, believing that they would be safer and much more comfortable aboard the "slightly injured liner" than in the small wooden boats. An unidentified passenger was quoted as having responded to the call to board the lifeboats by saying, "You don't catch me leaving a warm bed to go up on that cold deck at midnight; I know better than that!"

Mrs. Ida S. Hippach of Chicago, wife of a wealthy glass dealer, is thought to have been aboard lifeboat number six. When the *Titanic* and the mass of unfortunate passengers in the water were out of sight, she began to wonder audibly when—or whether—she'd ever see the light of another day. "Don't worry, madam," a veteran seaman told her. "First light comes very early—in about four hours." In one lifeboat the well-dressed Scottish countess of Rothes reportedly stayed at the tiller for several hours. Her fellow survivors lauded her as "being as plain as an old shoe." Gladys Cherry, her cousin and traveling companion, pulled an oar for more than an hour without a break. Mrs. Maggie Brown took command of a boat for a considerable period and barked orders at the sailors who were aboard, adding to the legend of "The Unsinkable Molly Brown."

Beesley, who had learned earlier how to evade measures designed to keep second-class passengers from mingling with those in first class, may have been one of the men in number ten. He lived because he jumped from the deck of the liner into the boat near its stern. Mrs. May Futrelle resisted efforts to put her into number thirteen and was forced into it by an officer of the ship.

Georgette Madill, age fifteen, was later identified in newspaper stories as "the principal heir to the estate of Judge George Madill, a prominent banker of St. Louis." This young lady, who had an allowance of seventy-five hundred dollars per year, briefly helped to pull an oar in number eleven. In contrast, those in lifeboat number five afterward said of yachtsman Frederick M. Hoyt, "Mr. Hoyt declined his turn at the oar, saying that the skin of his hands was very tender."

About two hours after the *Titanic* had sunk from view, Fifth Officer Harold G. Lowe noted that some of the boats were leaking badly. Taking charge as though he had experienced many a long bout with the cruel sea, he managed to get his vessel lashed to one whose bottom sloshed with water. Eventually at least five and perhaps six boats were secured to one another in an effort to keep all afloat.

With two of her sisters, Mrs. Charlotte Appleton occupied a boat that may have been number twelve. The trio had been in London for the funeral of a fourth member of the family, Lady Victor Drummond, and they chose the *Titanic* for no reason except that its schedule was convenient. Both Mr. and Mrs. Edwin N. Kimball were in another lifeboat, possibly number ten. According to a dispatch from Boston, the head of the piano company bearing his name and his wife had sailed from New York on March 6 for "rest and a complete change" in Europe. While searching for signs of the dawn that did not come for another three hours, Kimball and his wife tried to master the use of one of the vessel's oars.

Despite the fact that two different transfers of passengers took place between lifeboats some time after 3:00 A.M., the most newsworthy incident during the hours of darkness took place in lifeboat number one, which contained only a dozen people. Most of its passengers were members of the ship's crew who took turns at the oars. Desperately striving to have the boat move faster, Sir Cosmo Edmund Duff Gordon proposed giving each man five pounds to have them increase their rhythm. Drawing out a few small sheets of paper, he scribbled on each a promissory note in the sum of five pounds. Distributed among the seamen, this unexpected largesse had no significant impact upon the rhythm of their rowing, but it created a sensation on two continents when Duff Gordon was accused of having saved his life by means of bribery.

Another story behind the money paid to the crewmen in the lifeboat is based on a conversation between one of the ship's firemen, R. Pusey, and Duff Gordon. Reacting to some of the passengers' comments regarding the things they had lost with the sinking of the ship, Pusey pointed out, "Never mind that, you have saved your lives, but we have lost our kit, and the company won't give us any more. And what's more, our pay stops from tonight." Annoyed by the crewman's comments, Duff Gordon said, "Very well, I will give you a fiver each to start a new kit!" Afterward, when it was also pointed out that boat number one made no effort to pick up any other survivors from the water, Duff Gordon's payment to the crewmen looked more like a payoff than a gratuity.

Survivor Martha Stephenson of Philadelphia seems to have been one of the few persons who carried a timepiece with her into one of the lifeboats. She told reporters that she was in the boat for at least five hours.

With dawn beginning to break, the *Carpathia* arrived in the area and began to take on the survivors in the lifeboats. Most of the passengers in the first lifeboat she found climbed an iron ladder to the deck of the rescue vessel, but at least one survivor was too weak to climb and was lifted upward by means of a sling. For many of these persons, "the most harrowing four hours of their lives" ended in ecstasy combined with profound grief at the fate of loved ones they would never see again.

20

DAWN FOR SOME

THE *CARPATHIA*

FOURTH OFFICER Joseph G. Boxhall was in charge of lifeboat number two and had only one other man with him. Since it took many people to handle the oars with any effectiveness, the women aboard took turns at propelling the boat. Of his experience there, Lawrence Beesley said, "A green light burning in this boat all night was the greatest comfort to the rest of us who had nothing to steer by; although it meant little in the way of safety in itself, it was a point to which we could look."

Around 4:30 A.M. Beesley learned that the little green light meant a great deal more than he had realized earlier. A lookout on the thirteen-thousand-ton *Carpathia* spotted it from a considerable distance. Since it was very near the water, he knew that it was from one of the *Titanic*'s lifeboats.

Capt. Arthur H. Rostron barked an order, "Dead slow, straight ahead," and one of his officers sounded the liner's whistle. That sound was later described by someone aboard lifeboat number two as "the most absolutely heavenly music that the human ear ever hears."

Before the sound of the whistle died down, the helmsman found it impossible to proceed as ordered. An iceberg of some size lay dead ahead. Swinging around toward the south, within a quarter of an hour the liner had closed on boat number two. Twenty-three women and two men, all of them wet and cold, were soon aboard the rescue vessel. Physically and mentally exhausted, Boxhall was barely able to speak, but he managed a hoarse whisper in which he informed Rostron, "She went down shortly after 2:00 A.M." It was not necessary to mention the *Titanic* by name.

Although the sun had not yet appeared, the eerie predawn half-light was sufficient for Rostron and his crew to begin the task of

LIBRARY OF CONGRESS

The Carpathia was a Cunard liner en route to the Mediterranean when the ship's wireless operator intercepted the Titanic's distress call. Although she was fully loaded with passengers of her own, the ship's captain took every step possible to make Titanic's survivors comfortable and reversed his course for New York.

finding the other lifeboats. As the sun rose, many survivors were startled to see "debris of chairs, portions of several life jackets, and wreckage of all kinds." Clearly, they were not far from the spot at which the *Titanic* went down. The lifeboats had been rowing in circles for three or four hours.

Heart-wrenching as the floating debris was, the women and men in the small boats gave most of their attention to the ice, which seemed to have taken over the North Atlantic. Some large sheets appeared to loom six or eight feet above the water. After having counted thirty-one visible bergs, a few of which looked to be over one hundred feet tall, one woman wondered aloud, "How on earth did we fail to bump into one of them in the dark?" No one responded. Some of her companions were mesmerized, watching the floating ice change color from pink to gold and every hue in between.

To speed up the rescue operation, Rostron's men slung netting over the sides of their vessel. Most of the men were able to climb

---

TITANIC'S "C. Q. D." CAUGHT BY A LUCKY FLUKE

Carpathia's Wireless Man Had Finished Work For Night, But Going Back to Verify a " Time Rush " He Caught the Call For Help.

BY HAROLD THOMAS COTTAM, WIRELESS OPERATOR ON THE CARPATHIA.

The New York Times *bought the firsthand account of Harold Cottam, the Marconi operator aboard the* Carpathia, *as it had that of Harold Bride of the* Titanic.

up the netting or the iron ladder at the port side of the *Carpathia*. Numerous women and a few men were pulled aboard in boatswain's chairs and slings. For the smallest children, canvas bags securely tied to the ends of ropes were adequate.

According to Beesley, it was at least 8:30 A.M., or more than six hours after they took to the lifeboats, before the last survivors were aboard the rescue ship. They immediately received blankets and hot beverages. Meanwhile, the ship's officers wrote down their names and what class they had been in before directing them to quarters that had been made ready. The *Carpathia* could accommodate only one hundred first-class passengers and two hundred second-class, but her steerage was large enough to take care of more than two thousand passengers. The *Titanic*'s third-class passengers were sent below, along with members of the crew. First- and second-class passengers were assigned crowded but comfortable quarters. As the highest ranking surviving officer, Lightoller—who was the last person from the sunken liner to climb aboard the rescue vessel—was given an entire cabin. Every one of the *Carpathia*'s crewmen worked long hours trying to make the survivors as comfortable as possible.

Rostron ordered as many of the lifeboats stowed aboard as would fit. Six were added to *Carpathia*'s davits, seven were placed on the foredeck, and the other seven, including the collapsibles, were set adrift.

No one knew how many persons who had found places in the lifeboats had died during the hours of darkness. At least three bodies were left in the sinking Englehardt A when the other occupants crawled into Englehardt D. At least three more were dead when their lifeboats reached the *Carpathia*. In her log they were listed as: "W. H. Lyons, able-bodied seaman; S. C. Siebert, steward; apparently a fireman, identity unknown." When the ship reached the coordinates given in *Titanic*'s last message, Rostron assembled part of the ship's company and numerous survivors in the main lounge. Father Roger Anderson, an Anglican priest and a passenger aboard the *Carpathia*, conducted a brief funeral service, then the three bodies were buried at sea. "When it was over," Beesley wrote, "the ship steamed on to carry the living back to the land."

Precisely what land should be chosen as the destination of the liner was a matter of considerable concern. Halifax, Nova Scotia, was about as close as any other point, but that route was likely to have a great deal of ice. Having been headed to the Mediterranean, departing New York on Thursday, April 11, Rostron felt he could not entirely ignore the approximately 750 passengers he had aboard. After consulting some of the 126 who were in first class, he decided to return to New York.

The passengers aboard the *Carpathia* did whatever they could to help the crew and *Titanic*'s survivors. They provided extra clothes, shared their cabins, and donated their toiletries. They sewed smocks for the children and women, robbing their own steamer chests of whatever material they needed. They did their best to be cheerful and supportive, but the survivors held themselves back. It was not snobbery but rather shock. Whatever the survivors had experienced, the passengers on the *Carpathia*, regardless of the degree of sympathy, could never understand.

ONE MAN who left New York with the *Carpathia* was neither a member of the crew nor a passenger. Harold T. Cottam, age twenty-one, was employed by the Marconi Company to operate the liner's wireless system. Unlike the elegant wireless cabin of the *Titanic*, Cottam had a hastily improvised room aft of the funnel. Unfortunately, no relief operator was aboard.

Cottam played a key role in saving hundreds of lives, for after having communicated with Jack Phillips earlier on Sunday, he was about to go to bed when he remembered that he should transmit a reminder concerning the ice reports to the *Titanic*. After having tapped out the call letters of the *Carpathia*, MPA, he contacted his counterpart on the west-bound liner. To the larger vessel, or MGY, he planned to send word that a quantity of messages were being dispatched to the White Star vessel from Cape Cod, or MCC.

Barely having started his transmission, Cottam was interrupted by Phillips who tapped out: "Come at once we have hit a berg its CQD this time our position is 41°46'N by 50°14'W."

The last boat pulls alongside the Carpathia. *Boat number twelve was dangerously overcrowded after picking up thirty survivors from the overturned Collapsible B. By nine o'clock the last survivor was aboard the rescue ship.*

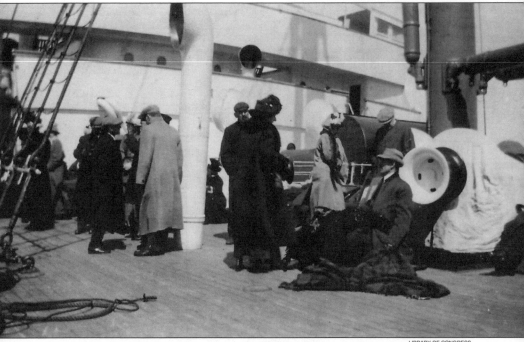

Survivors clustered on the deck of the Carpathia *en route to New York. The ship's original passengers spared no effort to accommodate their needs.*

The young Marconi operator found First Officer H. V. Dean, blurted out the situation, and with him hurried to Rostron's cabin. Initially nettled at being disturbed just as he was turning in for the night, the captain pulled on his clothes and went to the chart room as rapidly as possible. After a few moments, he announced that the position given to Cottam by the *Titanic* put the luxury liner approximately fifty-eight miles away.

Before his vessel changed her course in order to steam toward the damaged liner, Cottam returned to what he called his shack and took a flurry of brief messages that originated from both the *Titanic* and her sister vessel, the *Olympic*. Though much farther away from the scene of the collision with the iceberg than was the *Carpathia*, powerful wireless equipment on both White Star vessels enabled them to communicate. Despite having been requested to come immediately, with her boats ready, the *Olympic* was too far away to be of help.

When his firsthand experiences were published in the *Times* under his byline on April 19, Cottam's story was spread across five

Despite the best efforts of the Carpathia's *passengers, the* Titanic's *survivors remained separate and aloof, some finding loved ones thought lost but most mourning those who did not survive.*

columns. Readers learned that the last message he received from the *Titanic* just before midnight was, "Come quick. Our engine room is flooded up to the boilers."

In response to this message, Cottam "kept calling them to warn them to look out for our rockets, but I shall never know whether he heard me or not." Wearing his headset until his vessel came near the location reported to him from Phillips, Cottam said he never got a single spark from the emergency set of the *Titanic*.

Pushing through the night that was lighted only by stars and a thin crescent moon, the *Carpathia* reached her top speed and stayed there. Rostron later testified, "We never slackened, though sometimes we had to alter course to avoid icebergs. Beginning at 3:00 A.M., we fired rockets at fifteen-minute intervals. Just before 4:00 A.M. we reached the position at which the *Titanic* should have been found, but the sea was empty as far as we could see. Our vision was partly blocked by a huge berg that was moving so slowly it seemed to be standing still."

Carpathia's *captain, Arthur H. Rostron, was a deeply religious man. When he understood that he had 705 survivors aboard his vessel and 1,525 had perished, he called for a memorial service in the ship's lounge as they neared the site of the sinking.*

His heart heavy because he now knew that the *Titanic* was lost, Rostron turned his attention to the search for lifeboats. Not until hours after the last of them had been found did he try to tabulate the results of his race to the scene of the disaster. According to his officers, who had been told to "check and double-check as you identify survivors," the *Carpathia* had 705 survivors from the *Titanic* aboard. That meant the iceberg had resulted in the loss of about 1,525 lives. After formal hearings, the British Board of Trade reported 711 survivors. A reporter for the *Illustrated London News* was prompted to wonder whether or not officials "counted a few dead men as survivors, since some of them were taken aboard the rescue vessel."

Although Cottam was bone-tired when his ship reached the search area, he stayed at his post and within two hours after the first survivor was aboard he sent out his first list of survivors' names. Because his wireless system was far from the best, Cottam arranged to send messages to the *Olympic* for retransmission to Cape Race and other American stations. Soon the U.S. Navy's scout *Chester,* dispatched by the president, was in a good position to serve as a relay station. Unfortunately her wireless operator was branded by Cottam as "insufferably incompetent."

In time, names were handed to Cottam much more rapidly than he could transmit them. At the point of collapse, he sent word to the *Titanic's* surviving operator, Harold Bride, that he was desperately in need of help. Although Bride's feet had been frostbitten in the lifeboat, he agreed and was carried into the wireless room, where he took over and worked until Cottam had rested sufficiently to resume his task. Following a directive from Rostron, both operators aboard the *Carpathia* pushed aside Marconigrams received from shore and made no attempt to respond to them. Many inquiries came from newspapers in New York, Boston, Philadelphia, and other cities. Numerous anxious messages were received from relatives and friends of persons known to have been traveling first class on the *Titanic.* President William Howard Taft was among those who were anxious for word, since his confidant Maj. Archibald Butt was aboard the ill-fated liner. Taft was treated like everyone else on shore except White Star executives; his wireless inquiries, dispatched one after another, brought no reply.

The first brief list of survivors that appeared in the *New York Times* was far from complete, with names misspelled or incomplete. Only a few days later the newspaper gave the world a list that was almost as accurate as any that has been compiled during

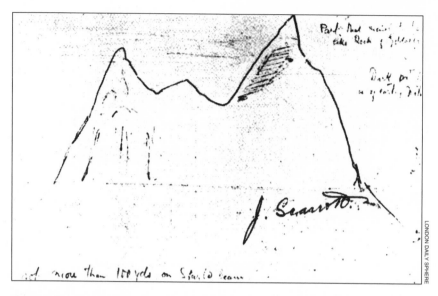

One of the ship's crew sketched the iceberg he glimpsed just prior to the collision. Note the similarity to the iceberg photographed from the German liner Prinze Adelbert *on page 74.*

later decades. As was the custom, persons in first class were given prominence. Since virtually all members of the crew were British citizens, their names were not published in the United States. Lightoller was annoyed at this omission, since he had supervised the careful compilation of their names and he had expected American newspapers to transmit them to British publications. It was weeks before the names of surviving able-bodied seamen, trimmers, greasers, stokers, cooks, messmen, stewards, elevator operators, and bell boys were made public.

In New York, hundreds of relatives and friends had arrived to embrace the survivors or to search for those whose names were not listed among the survivors but who might have been overlooked or their names misunderstood. A few came because of second-class passengers, but most were concerned about someone in first class. There is no record that public interest was shown in the largest group of men, women, and children who had set out to make the crossing—the passengers in steerage.

21

ALL THE NEWS
THAT'S FIT TO PRINT

FACTS AND FANTASIES

CARR VAN Anda always scanned news bulletins taken from the air but usually put them aside quickly. On the morning of Monday, April 15, he read and reread an Associated Press dispatch based upon several ship-to-shore communications. He closed his eyes, meditated briefly, then called in his staff.

"A bulletin has been picked up," he informed them, "according to which the *Titanic* has hit an iceberg and has been gravely injured. I believe it reached the mainland by way of the liner *Olympic*, but I am not positive. Soon we'll be on deadline. Here are your assignments."

One man was sent to the newspaper's morgue, where photos were filed, to find images of each notable known to be aboard the liner. A colleague led a team to assemble biographical profiles of as many of these as possible.

Although rapid action was essential if the early edition was to give as much information as possible about the vessel and her occupants, Van Anda was not ready to go with the story until he received confirmation. One staffer was instructed to contact a *Times* correspondent in Quebec, and another hurried off to try to reach their man in Montreal. "Don't fail to get in touch with Halifax," the managing editor called to both of them. Three reporters were assigned the job of checking with the wireless stations along the coast to see what word, if any, they had received. Several men were told to get on the telephone, roust every *Times* employee who could be found, and instruct him to hurry to the newspaper's building on Times Square.

When portions of the messages that had been exchanged between the Marconi operators aboard the *Titanic* and the

"All the News That's Fit to Print."	**The New York Times.**	THE WEATHER.

VOL. LXI...NO. 19,502.   NEW YORK, TUESDAY, APRIL 16, 1912—TWENTY-FOUR PAGES.   ONE CENT

TITANIC SINKS FOUR HOURS AFTER HITTING ICEBERG; 866 RESCUED BY CARPATHIA, PROBABLY 1250 PERISH; ISMAY SAFE, MRS. ASTOR MAYBE, NOTED NAMES MISSING

The New York Times *scored a major journalistic coup by being the first to put together the story of the sinking of the* Titanic.

Carpathia were found, the newspaper editor took these as confirmation of the brief bulletin he had received earlier. He then called for all file material on the White Star Line and its vessels, executives, and ships' captains.

When the early morning edition of the *Times* rolled off the press, page one carried headlines unlike any other newspaper in the United States or England. A photograph of the *Titanic* and one of Capt. Edward J. Smith added touches of authenticity. Numerous page-one stories jumped inside the newspaper, whose first six pages were devoted almost entirely to the *Titanic*—756 column inches in all.

At 10:55 P.M. (ship's time) on Sunday, readers learned, wireless exchanges among the *Titanic,* the *Olympic,* and the *Baltic* were picked up by the Allan liner *Virginian.* Bound for Liverpool out of Halifax, she relayed some of these messages to Halifax. Since the *Virginian* was a small mail boat, her passenger agent was of the opinion that she would have been unable to help the world's largest cruiser. Sir Montague Allan, head of the line bearing his name, was contacted in London. He told the *Times:* "We have had no word from the Virginian, and have received no official messages as to the whereabouts of the passengers [on the *Titanic*]. We have received, however, a Marconigram dispatched to New York stating that the Carpathia arrived on the spot where the Titanic had been, that all of the Titanic's boats had been accounted for, and that 666 of the passengers had been saved, but that the rest had gone down with the Titanic. This is not official and we have no official news yet. I shall be very glad to make public the text of any official news we receive."

All steamers of the undermentioned Lines will follow the NEW SOUTHERLY COURSE Eastbound and Westbound, thus avoiding all possibility of meeting ice, and each steamer will have BOAT AND LIFE RAFT capacity for every person on board, including both passengers and crew.

New 45,000 Ton **OLYMPIC** Sails from NEW YORK **MAY 25** JUNE 13—JULY 6 JULY 27—AUG. 17

American Line
N.Y.—Plymouth—Cherbourg—Southampton
Philadelphia, May 11, New York, May 25
Philadelphia—Queenstown—Liverpool.
Haverford, May 4, Merion, May 18.

White Star Line
N.Y.—Plymouth—Cherbourg—Southampton
*Philadelphia, May 11, Oceanic, May 18.
*American Line Steamer.
New York—Queenstown—Liverpool
Baltic ....May 9 | Cedric, May......16
Boston—Queenstown—Liverpool
Arabic...May 7 | Cymric (2d class) May 22
FROM TO **Mediterranean**
BOSTON THE
Cretic ......May 18 | Canopic ....June 8

Red Star Line
N.Y.—London—Paris via Dover—Antwerp
Finland, May 4, Vaderland, May 11.

Atlantic Transport Line
New York—London Direct.
Minnetonka, May 4. Minnehaha, May 11.

WHITE STAR LINE
CANADIAN SERVICE
LARGEST STEAMERS FROM CANADA
From Montreal via Quebec to Liverpool
MEGANTIC   May 11,   June 8,   July 6
*TEUTONIC   May 18,   June 15,   July 13
LAURENTIC   May 25,   June 22,   July 20
*CANADA ....June 1,   June 29, .July 27
*Only One Class of Cabin (II) Passengers

ROBT. E. M. BAIN, S. W. Pass. Agt. Both Phones, 9th and Locust Sts., St. Louis, Mo.

Some of the New York newspapers whose headlines proclaimed the sinking of the Titanic *also carried advertisements for the next crossing of her sister ship, the* Olympic.

Although two-thirds of the *Times* news-gathering staff was racing to put together what amounted to a special edition, they knew Van Anda was proceeding upon unofficial news. A few hours hence, official news might be received that the *Titanic* was sailing serenely toward New York.

Because he risked his job, the managing editor of the *Times* achieved what every newsman dreams of accomplishing: he had a scoop on the most dramatic story of the era. One page carried photographs of the luxurious Parisian Café, the restaurant reception room, and the first-class smoking room of the *Titanic,* plus a view of a "First Class State Room." Most of these pictures, sent to the *Times* earlier by White Star executives eager for free publicity, had been photographed aboard the *Olympic* rather than the *Titanic*. The two liners were virtually identical in many respects, and since the *Olympic* was launched earlier, it was much more extensively photographed.

A cluster of illustrations depicted what *Times* staffers called "Rescuing Fleet and One of the Commanders." Rostron of the *Carpathia* was incorrectly identified as "Capt. Ranson" under a photo acquired from the American Press Association. Along with the *Carpathia*, the other "rescue vessels" depicted were the *Baltic*, *Virginian*, *Olympic*, and *Parisian*. That four of the five played no part in the actual rescue work was a minor gaffe that was completely overshadowed by the fact that no competitor of the *Times* had any account at all of the disaster in its early edition.

Since the cream of American society was aboard the vessel, it was relatively easy for Van Anda's staffers to put together "Some of the Notable Passengers Who Were on Board the Titanic." This photo spread depicted nine men: Henry B. Harris, Maj. Archibald Butt, Col. W. Roebling, J. M. C. Smith, Isidor Straus, J. B. Thayer, F. D. Millet, B. Guggenheim, and J. J. Astor. Ladies whose photos appeared included Mrs. G. D. Widener and Mrs. J. J. Astor. Of the men, only Smith survived, and both women reached New York as widows.

A photograph of the *Titanic* that ran across the entire top of a page gave readers many of the vital statistics of the "Largest Steamship Ever Launched":

Length overall, 882 feet, 5 inches
Breadth overall, 92 feet 6 inches
Breadth over boat deck, 94 feet
Height from bottom of keel to top of captain's house, 105 feet
    7 inches
Height of funnels above casing, 72 feet
Height of funnels above boat deck, 81 feet 5 inches
Distance from top of funnel to keel, 175 feet
Number of steel decks, 11
Number of watertight bulkheads, 15
Passengers accommodated, 2,500
Crew, 860
Tonnage, registered, 45,000
Tonnage, displacement, 66,000
Approximate cost, $7,500,000

From the wireless station at Cape Race, a message from the *Carpathia* that was relayed to Newfoundland by the *Olympic* gave a brief list of known survivors. "The Marconi station reports that it missed the word after 'Mrs. Jacob P.' readers were informed. At the *Times*, it was surmised—correctly as it proved later—that the name should have read "Mrs. J. J. Astor" since "except for

On the streets of London the unbelievable news called for special broadsides.

Mrs. H. J. Allison, Mrs. Astor is the only lady in the 'A' column of the ship's passenger list accompanied by a maid."

A lengthy newspaper story appeared under the headline: LONDON WENT TO BED THINKING ALL SAVED. At Halifax, a *Times* correspondent consulted unidentified maritime officials and from them learned that charts suggested the Atlantic Ocean was at least two miles deep at the point where the *Titanic* sank. A special bulletin from Washington summarized the views of naval constructor David W. Taylor, who was of the opinion that the watertight bulkheads of the *Titanic* had somehow failed. Not until much later was it discovered that they failed, not because they were weak, but because they did not extend all the way to the tops of the compartments.

A majority of newspaper editors faced the dilemma that confronted Van Anda and came to different decisions. In its final edition of April 15, New York's *Evening Sun* reported that the *Titanic* was lost but no one had died. The following day, after the *Times* had published its first estimate of casualties, the *Evening Sun* remained confident that all passengers were safe.

Much the same mood prevailed throughout the nation. Editors of the highly respected *Christian Science Monitor* told readers that the *Titanic*'s passengers were on the way to Halifax aboard two steamers and that the damaged liner was being towed to the same port by the *Virginian*. In Roanoke, Virginia, the *Evening News* acknowledged that "a fearful accident" had put two thousand lives in danger. With "an awful calamity" apparently impending, readers of this newspaper were told that "later reports show that all on board were saved." In London, the *Daily Mail* also acknowledged on April 16 that the *Titanic* was lost but stated that no lives had been lost.

Some fantasies probably stemmed from the fact that White Star officials did not budge in their assertion that all was well. Long after some rivals of the *Times* belatedly followed its lead and told readers that there had been tremendous loss of life, at the New York office of the steamship company, vice president Philip A. S. Franklin stoutly insisted that no disaster had occurred. Even a *Times* reporter swallowed an account that was received from Saint John's, Newfoundland. According to a dispatch that originated there, no word of the disaster had reached shore from the liner *Carpathia,* known to be little more than fifty miles from the scene of the purported disaster. "It is certain," said a small story deep inside the *Times,* "that had any boat been near enough to the Titanic to learn definitely of her sinking, the Carpathia would have been that boat."

Many of the fantastic accounts that went into print stemmed from editorial acceptance of wireless messages. Some were garbled and misleading. Others seem to have originated with pranksters who thought it great fun to transmit refutations of serious operators. In New York, a man identified himself as the chairman of the Marconi Company of the United States and complained to a *Times* reporter that his operators "had been subjected to interference by unrecognized stations."

So many bogus dispatches were received that officials of the Justice Department in Washington were said to be preparing a special investigative body. These detectives, *Times* readers were told, would be detailed "to run down the men who sent the [false] messages and the local stations from which the flashes started." An unnamed official told reporters that talk of "amateurs amusing themselves at public expense" was nonsense. The real motive for sending out fabricated messages, he said, was "to postpone knowledge of the wreck in order to give time for the reinsuring of the Titanic's cargo."

C. W. Bennet, British consul general in New York, took erroneous or falsified wireless dispatches so seriously that he reported them to his foreign secretary, Sir Edward Grey. Bennet blamed bogus news on "the improper use of wireless by unauthorized amateurs who picked up parts of messages" and pieced them together. He stressed that at least one message was clearly forged. "Purporting to come from Mr. Phillips, the wireless operator of the *Titanic,*" it was sent to his mother. All was well, Phillips is supposed to have assured her; "vessel now proceeding to Halifax."

At White Star offices in New York, vice president Franklin finally confessed that there had been a tremendous loss of life. A dispatch from Capt. Herbert J. Haddock of the *Olympic* eventually led Franklin to admit that the *Titanic* was not being towed to Halifax by the *Virginian.* Calling Haddock's message very brief, the executive said, "It neglected to mention that all of the crew had been saved." Anxious inquiries at the office of the steamship line brought responses that "the *Titanic* would reach port, under her own steam probably, but surely with the help of the Allan liner *Virginian.*"

Years later, looking back at the chaotic hours in which many wild guesses about the *Titanic* got into print, journalist Michael W.

Jones pointed out that the majority of editors who put out bulletins about the ship's collision with the iceberg flanked it with reports about her invulnerability. "Alone, in splendid isolation," he concluded, "the *New York Times* grasped the nettle in both hands by categorically affirming the liner had sunk."

22

PIER FIFTY-FOUR

AGONY AND ECSTASY

ON THE morning of April 16, fresh word about the disaster at sea was received at an unlikely place. The management of Wanamaker's department store in New York believed that their clientele—both local and out of town—liked to be informed about new things. A few months earlier, they had decided that wireless radio "looked like a coming thing." Hence a working Marconi station was installed in the building and given the call letters MHI. Placards throughout the store invited patrons to visit the top floor, watch the Marconi apparatus at work, and even send or receive a message.

Like the three operators on the *Titanic* and the *Carpathia*, the man at the key of the Wanamaker's station was young—just twenty-one years old. Born in Minsk, Russia, he came to the United States at the age of nine and became interested in wireless radio very early. A highly skilled operator who seldom made the kind of mistakes that were plaguing the newspapers that day with omitted words and misspelled names, David Sarnoff had come to work early that morning. He soon began catching messages from a variety of stations, all of which had the same theme—unmitigated disaster. Word garnered from the air by Sarnoff was a vindication of the *New York Times*, which had printed the tragic story first, and a source of humiliation to the editors of the rival *Evening Sun* that had not.

Eighteen years after having played a little known but important role in the *Titanic* disaster, Sarnoff became president of the Radio Corporation of America. This enterprise bought out the Marconi Company of the United States and was itself later absorbed by the General Electric Company.

The New York Times.

VOL. LXI...NO. 19,808.   • • •   NEW YORK, THURSDAY, APRIL 18, 1912.—TWENTY-FOUR PAGES.   ONE CENT

CARPATHIA HERE TO-NIGHT WITH TITANIC'S SURVIVORS; HER REPORTS SHOW 700 SAVED; 1,500 GONE TO DEATH; WIRELESS MERELY OUTLINES THE TRAGIC STORY

News of the rescue performed by the Carpathia *brought thousands to the shipyard to witness the debarkation of the* Titanic's *survivors.*

LARGELY AS a reaction to the attention-riveting issue of the *Times,* residents of the city who knew that relatives or friends were on the *Titanic* besieged the offices of the White Star Line. "By 8 o'clock offices of the steamship line were crowded from booking rail to booking rail," the *Times* reported. Inside two large offices of the International Mercantile Marine, the newspaper said, "men and women with eyes red from weeping were banked in between the long booking desks. Sometimes a grief stricken cry followed the giving of information. On one or two occasions when the news was good, there was a hysterical joyous expression of relief. Outside on the opposite side of Broadway and filling Bowling Green Park was another crowd, in which could be seen many a tear-streaked face. The crowd increased in size so rapidly that the four policemen detailed to duty in front of the steamship offices asked for reinforcements."

By late afternoon anxiety or sorrow pervaded many a household. Telegraph offices were overwhelmed by the traffic from persons desperate for the latest word about the mighty vessel and its occupants. Dozens of persons were packing to travel or were already on their way to New York to seek information in person.

Solomon Guggenheim, Mr. and Mrs. Robert Guggenheim, Nettie Gerstle, and Louis Rothschild had attended a Broadway play. Emerging from the theater, apparently without having seen a newspaper during the day, they learned "the shocking news" and hurried to the White Star offices. Despite their influence, the Guggenheims were unable to get any word except that 675 persons from the *Titanic* were reportedly now aboard the *Carpathia.*

A late edition of the *Times* described growing pandemonium at White Star offices. Philip A. S. Franklin, the U.S. vice president of the line, told frantic relatives that he was doing his best but he

Anxious for news of the survivors, family members and friends converged on White Star's offices in New York each day until the Carpathia arrived. Early reports of the tragedy had been confused and garbled, but later questions centered on who had survived.

could not be certain that the *Times* was accurate. Late in the afternoon, he came from his office to tell a crowd of relatives packed into a reception room that he had been unable to make contact with the ship *Parisian* or with the *Virginian*. Himself frantic by this time, he was forced to concede that a wireless "seeming to have originated with Capt. Herbert J. Haddock of White Star's *Olympic* was discouraging to those who hoped that the *Parisian* and the *Virginia* had reached the site" where the *Titanic* experienced trouble.

Franklin instructed members of his staff to stress that "first hand knowledge will not be available until the *Carpathia* reaches this city, hopefully on Thursday night but possibly not until Friday morning." To an aide, the steamship company executive mused that "Capt. Smith, I am sure, went down with his ship. Capt. Haddock had no word of him, but I know Capt. Smith. He is that kind of a man."

About 11:00 P.M. frantic inquirers received what the *Times* described the next day as "a ray of hope." A Marconigram from Sable Island, perhaps the land station closest to the scene of the collision with an iceberg, noted that it was very difficult to deliver names of survivors correctly. "Passengers are believed dispersed among several vessels," the operator explained. Still, one question was on everyone's mind: "How could the *Titanic* sink?"

By late afternoon Franklin's first public message about the vessel and its voyage had been removed from bulletin boards. Hours after the special edition of the *Times* was out, the White Star and International Mercantile Marine executive had posted a notice that read in part: "While no direct messages have been received from the Titanic, officials are perfectly satisfied that there is no cause for alarm concerning the safety of the passengers or the ship, as they regard the Titanic as being practically unsinkable. They do not regard the cessation of the ship's wireless messages as anything serious, as this might have been caused by atmospheric disturbances or other causes. The Titanic is well able to withstand almost any exterior damage and could keep afloat indefinitely after being struck."

Relatively few members of the general public learned that still another wireless message, allegedly relayed by way of the *Olympic*, offered no hope at all. "Loss likely total, 1,800 souls," the Marconigram read. Coming from an unidentified station, it was checked against all information from Cape Race and from ships known to have had even brief contact with the *Titanic*. Although the sender could not be identified and the dreadful news could not be verified, those who learned of it were described as "going through paroxysms of total emotional agony."

Some of the anxious families had some comfort from the *Times* headline: RULE OF SEA FOLLOWED. That implied that all women and children were put over in lifeboats and thus were "supposed to be safe."

Charles Sumner, general manager of the Cunard Line to which the *Carpathia* belonged, received no word from the vessel after she passed beyond range of Cape Race and Sable Island. He expected but did not get Marconigrams from a station somewhat closer to New York. To inquirers whose faces showed the agony they were experiencing, he explained that the wireless equipment on the rescue ship had a range of only about two hundred miles. When a reporter asked when the *Carpathia* was expected at New York, "he said with much feeling that he could not even find out where she

Even after the Carpathia *docked at pier fifty-four, wireless operators Cottam and Bride were still transmitting personal messages from the survivors and a list of the passengers and crew lost at sea. At the foot of the gangway stood an imposing army of newspaper reporters and Sen. William Alden Smith.*

was." He did venture to guess that the *Carpathia* must have been "within sixty or seventy miles of the Titanic when the latter vessel struck the iceberg."

On Thursday the anxious nation learned that Treasury Department officials in Washington had given orders "to expedite in every way the landing of the survivors of the Titanic and to aid them in meeting their friends on the arrival of the Carpathia." Custom regulations were suspended and officers of that service were ordered to help survivors make speedy contact with persons searching for them.

Following instructions from Washington, barricades were erected to cordon off Fourteenth Street as far east as Eighth Avenue. Inspector George McCluskey of the New York City police department took charge of nearly two hundred men whose duty it was to maintain order. A special detail of detectives was sent out "as a precaution against the work of pickpockets and petty thieves."

Still obeying instructions from Washington, police roped off a space more than 150 feet wide at the base of Cunard's pier number fifty-four. Close to the waterline, large letters of the alphabet were placed on poles. Only two persons seeking a given survivor were permitted inside this area, and they were instructed to stand in the line whose letter was the first in the survivor's surname.

Newspaper executives were angered when they were told that reporters would not receive passes to enter the roped-off area. Mayor W. J. Gaynor issued a special directive to police commissioner Rhinelander Waldo: "On the arrival of the Carpathia with its survivors you will exclude all photographers from the pier space devoted to the Custom Service. You will exclude all photographers or picture takers from entrance to the rest of the pier. Also rope off a large space on the outside for the protection of these unfortunate people from all approach or interference of photographers or any one else. We owe this to them, and let it be carried out strictly."

At least one editor guessed aloud, correctly as he later learned, that "Morgan and the Astors are behind this." Having no other choice, all New York and some out-of-town newspapers rented hotel rooms as close to the point of debarkation as possible. They then set up direct telephone lines linking these rooms with their editorial offices.

When the pilot vessel *New York* left her berth, her movement was correctly interpreted as a signal that the *Carpathia* would soon be guided to her dock. A handful of reporters and photographers handed out bribes freely and managed to board the *New York*. As

An artist's conception of the welcome given the Titanic's *survivors includes the three possibilities of the one who survived to be greeted by his loved ones, the survivors who had lost a loved one in the sinking, and the families whose loved ones did not survive.*

soon as the rescue ship was met, magnesium flares began going off while reporters used megaphones to shout questions.

A thunderstorm poured on the estimated thirty thousand people massed beyond the police lines as the *Carpathia* deposited the lifeboats from the *Titanic* in an area used by the White Star Line before docking itself at the Cunard pier. Canopied gangways were put in place, and the *Carpathia*'s passengers were allowed to disembark first. Well after 9:00 P.M. on Thursday, April 18, survivors from first class began coming down gangways and were welcomed by tumultuous shouts. After greeting their relatives, they were guided to a line of cars. A few, J. Bruce Ismay among them, went to luxury hotels. New Yorkers went home. Other survivors were taken to hotels rented by the White Star Line or to nearby hospitals.

For some the climactic appearance of a loved one meant that the ordeal was over, but for many a time of mourning was just

These two waifs were unidentified at the time they arrived in New York. Their father had been traveling under an alias, and so it took weeks to establish their identities and reunite them with their mother.

NEW YORK HERALD

beginning. At Grand Central Station, the widow of Charles Hays boarded a special train that took her to Canada. Some citizens of Philadelphia accepted the offer of free transportation home on a special train provided by the Pennsylvania Railroad. Wealthy members of the city's elite were aboard private trains before 11:00 P.M.

About the time the trains began to pull out of Penn Station, the *Titanic*'s steerage passengers started to leave the *Carpathia*. Most of these people, about 176 in number, went to shelters that had been hastily provided by the American Red Cross. It took more than half an hour for these immigrants, nearly all of whom spoke little or no English, to clear the rescue ship.

Finally, members of the crew, whose pay had stopped at midnight Sunday, were guided to the Immigration Service tender *George Starr* and transported to an awaiting International Mercantile Marine vessel. Once aboard the *Lapland*, the four officers of the *Titanic* were shown to their cabins, the two hundred remaining crew members were sent into steerage space, and the ship soon departed for England.

23

HALIFAX

MISSION MACABRE

A BULLETIN from Halifax, Nova Scotia, was published in numerous newspapers on April 16, which briefly buoyed the spirits of nearly everyone whose mind was fixed upon the *Titanic*. The source of the information was never discovered. The unsigned dispatch reported:

> Held afloat only by her watertight compartments, the great White Star liner Titanic is slowly crawling toward this harbor. Her passengers have been taken aboard the Cunard liner Carpathia and the Parisian of the Allan line only to have to face a second ordeal as they are to be again transferred to the Baltic of the White Star line this afternoon. The Baltic will take them to their journey's end in New York, where they are due Thursday.
>
> The disaster to the Titanic is unparalleled in the history of navigation. The largest, most luxurious, and best appointed liner ever laid down, she seemed proof against any disaster. Hardly another craft afloat could have withstood the terrific shock when the Titanic, driving along at better than half speed although in the midst of ice fields, crashed bow on into a great submerged mountain of ice which tore away her steel plates.

A second special dispatch from Canso, Nova Scotia, which modified and amplified that news, informed readers:

> The White Star liner Titanic, having transferred her passengers to the Parisian and Carpathia, was, at 2 o'clock this afternoon being towed to Halifax by the Virginian of the Allan line.

The Virginian passed a line to the Titanic as soon as the passengers had been transferred, and the latest word received by wireless was that there was no doubt that the new White Star liner would reach port. Agents of the White Star line at Halifax have been ordered to have wrecking tugs sent out to aid the Virginian with her tow into port.

AT HIS New York office, Phillip A. S. Franklin relied heavily upon these messages in his decision to dismiss the ominous news headlined in the *New York Times*. Believing that fifteen hundred travelers had been diverted to Nova Scotia, Franklin felt it imperative to get them to New York in more comfort than they would have aboard his line's little *Baltic,* and so he chartered a train of the New Haven Railroad and had it prepared to go to Halifax. Relatives and friends with whom White Star personnel could make contact were invited to travel on it, and many of them planned to make the trip. Franklin hoped that their train would reach the port before the arrival of the Cunard liner carrying the *Titanic*'s passengers.

In Washington the news from Nova Scotia was regarded with skepticism; no newspaper put the bulletins on page one. This editorial decision rested partly on the fact that at the State Department a special report was received from Ottawa, Canada, stating that officials there at the Marine Department believed the *Titanic* had sunk and that hundreds of her passengers had perished. They held out little hope that any bodies would be washed upon Canadian shores, as the Gulf Stream would carry them southward. "The Government service contains no boats large enough to proceed to the scene of the disaster," the officials explained. Yet they informed the Americans, "Orders will be issued for shore establishments to post scouts in hope of picking up bodies if by any chance they are washed onto the Canadian coast."

Consulted by U.S. State Department officials, experts in the U.S. Navy scoffed at the idea that casualties would be washed upon Canadian beaches. "Given the fact that the temperature of the salt water where the *Titanic* went down was below freezing," they pointed out, "many bodies would probably sink immediately and not come to the surface for days, if ever." If Franklin was aware of the views held in Washington, he ignored them.

In Chicago and other cities at a distance from New York, composers and songwriters were already busy. Some of them insisted that their only desire was to "commemorate the valiant dead," but

When the macabre mission to recover the bodies was being organized, undertakers from Canada's Maritime Provinces converged on Halifax to board the cable-laying ships Mackay-Bennett *and* Minia.

cynics argued that they actually wanted to cash in on the catastrophe. An early effort by Jeanette Forrest, entitled "The Wreck of the Titanic," was published by Frank K. Root and Company of Chicago. Numerous other special compositions and songs soon appeared; eventually these "musical tributes" exceeded two hundred in number.

Although the New Haven Railroad had prepared the special train composed largely of sleeper cars, Franklin reluctantly canceled it before it departed for Halifax. The evidence of the tragedy had become too overwhelming to ignore. He admitted that the only known survivors were aboard the *Carpathia* and were headed toward New York.

IT IS not known who originated the idea for the macabre mission, but on April 15 agents for the White Star Line chartered the only vessel of any size available in Halifax, the *Mackay-Bennett,* and dispatched it to the scene of the wreck to recover the bodies of the victims of the sinking.

The vessel departed at noon on April 17—hours before the *Titanic* survivors reached New York—with tons of ice, embalming supplies, and one hundred coffins. The Marconi equipment aboard the *Mackay-Bennett* was severely limited in range, but its operator

NOVA SCOTIA PUBLIC ARCHIVES

Very few photographs were taken of the recovery effort to retrieve the bodies of those Titanic *passengers who had died at sea. This image of workers from the* Minia *pulling a body from the water has no counterpart.*

sent out a general call. Ships within what was called "speaking distance" were queried for information on whatever wreckage and bodies they might have encountered in the area.

News of the disaster had already shifted the shipping lanes sixty miles farther south as ship traffic desired to give the scene of *Titanic*'s sinking a wide berth. There was also a preference to avoid the debris and bodies. Some ships, however, could not avoid the area, and their messages helped to guide the *Mackay-Bennett* to the scene.

Darkness fell as the cable-layer came close to the area in which wreckage had been spotted from other vessels, and so the work did not begin until Sunday morning. As was noted previously, fifty-one bodies were recovered and cataloged on the first day. Those bodies that had been disfigured by the week's exposure to the elements were given burials at sea.

A second vessel, the *Minia*, arrived on April 26 and assumed the recovery operation to allow the *Mackay-Bennett* to return to port with 190 bodies. The *Minia* remained in the area until May 3. The two ships recovered 323 bodies, and another 119 were buried at sea.

In Halifax tentative arrangements had been made for burial space in two cemeteries, and several railroads had indicated their readiness to transport many of the dead to their hometowns. A skating rink was converted into a makeshift morgue. Bodies believed to be those of first-class passengers were hauled in wooden coffins by teams of horses from the ships to the rink; canvas bags served for all others. Bodies not previously identified were checked and photographed before relatives were permitted to view them.

Within three days of the return of the *Mackay-Bennett* the burials began. The vast majority of those brought to Halifax were interred in one of three cemeteries—Fairview, a nonsectarian burial yard; Baron de Hirsch cemetery, a Jewish graveyard; and Mount Olivet, a Roman Catholic cemetery—but an estimated sixty coffins were shipped to the victims' homes, and most of them went to U.S. cities. The body of second-class passenger William Carbines was claimed by his two brothers and taken back to England. The body of one immigrant, Sigurd H. Moen, recrossed the Atlantic for burial in Bergen, Norway.

A bizarre chain of events revolved around a corpse identified as that of a Rochester, New York, traveling salesman. A woman identified as Lydia, a sister of Stanley H. Fox, explained that she had come to Halifax because the widow of the dead man could not travel as she was too grief-stricken. Lydia Fox then took care to see that the remains of her brother were properly stored in a baggage compartment and she then boarded the train. Soon thereafter a telegram arrived from Mrs. Cora Fox, warning authorities to be wary of a woman calling herself Lydia. Regarding Fox's remains, the message concluded, "Do not let her have the body."

When the train stopped at Truro, authorities removed the coffin and returned it to Halifax. Placed in storage, it remained there until the mayor of Rochester demanded that it be immediately shipped to Mrs. Fox in that city. Since the woman calling herself Lydia did not know of the actions taken at Truro, she continued her journey and was never heard of again. In Halifax, White Star agents speculated that "Lydia" might have been involved in some kind of insurance fraud.

On June 12, two days short of two months after the *Titanic* scraped the iceberg, the body of steward James McGrady was

Vincent Astor went to Halifax to claim his father's body. John Jacob Astor's body was the first to be identified and the first to be released to a victim's family.

interred in Fairview Cemetery in Halifax. That ended the formal involvement of the Nova Scotia port and at least five of her vessels in one of the most gruesome maritime searches on record.

The White Star Line established a trust fund for the perpetual care of the graves in the Fairview and Mount Olivet cemeteries. The congregation of Beth Israel synagogue in Halifax tended the graves in Baron de Hirsch. The Cunard Line assumed responsibility for the graves in the 1930s, when it acquired the White Star Line.

Nearly one-fourth of those lost at sea had been accounted for, thanks to the work of the ships and men from Nova Scotia. After no other shipwreck in history had such a large proportion of those who had died hundreds of miles from land been given respectable burial.

24

WILLIAM A. SMITH

BULLY PULPIT!

A MONG SOME politicians in Washington, the *Titanic* disaster was immediately seen as an opportunity to boost their prestige. One member of the House of Representatives borrowed a phrase from Theodore Roosevelt and said he was sure that an inquiry would provide someone with "a bully pulpit." Rep. Luther W. Mott of New York prepared a resolution calling for an investigation by the House Committee on Merchant Marine and Fisheries, but a backlog of business made it impossible for it to reach the floor.

Meanwhile, Sen. William Alden Smith of Michigan arranged to see President William Howard Taft for a few moments before going to the office of Attorney General George W. Wickersham. He then drafted a measure calling for action by the Senate Committee on Commerce, of which he was the ranking member. Although Smith did not know it, Sen. George G. Perkins of California had been preparing a bill that would require every vessel clearing an American port to be equipped with adequate lifeboats.

Smith was considering a run for the presidency in 1916, and he knew that the man who headed an inquiry into the loss of the *Titanic* would be in the headlines for weeks. He consulted a few other senators, who told him that his seniority guaranteed the passage some time the next day of a measure he had framed. Judging "time to be of the essence," reported the *New York Times,* Smith left the measure with a close friend and boarded the 3:30 P.M. train for New York that was known as The Congressional Limited.

Numerous other politicians saw in the disaster the same opportunity that Smith sensed. Half a dozen members of the House managed to see Judge Joshua W. Alexander of Missouri, who served as chairman of the merchant marine committee. Representatives from at least four widely separated states—Georgia, Indiana, New York, and Wisconsin—bombarded the committee chairman. Each had his own ideas about the focus of a formal inquiry as well as the makeup of an investigative body. So did Alexander. When he learned that while the Mott resolution was languishing in the House, the Smith request was moving rapidly toward the floor of the Senate, Alexander scrapped plans for action by the House of Representatives.

As Smith expected, the request went to the Commerce Committee, where it was quickly approved with only minor changes. Moving to the floor, it was adopted by voice vote of the senators during the morning session of April 17. Perkins of California, Jonathan Bourne of Oregon, Theodore Burton of Ohio, Furnifold M. Simmons of North Carolina, Francis G. Newlands of Nevada, and Duncan U. Fletcher of Florida were named to serve on what came to be popularly known as "the *Titanic* subcommittee" headed by Smith.

That afternoon, the *Times* reported:

> Survivors of the Titanic disaster will be summoned to tell the facts concerning the inability of the steamship officials to save the lives of all the passengers on the great liner. J. Bruce Ismay, Managing Director of the White Star Line, who is one of the survivors, will be asked to relate his story of the disaster. He will be questioned particularly respecting the facilities of the Titanic for the rescue of passengers, crew, and officers, and such matters that it is important for Congress to know, with the view to their utilization in the enactment of legislation amendatory of the ocean navigation laws of the United States.

Senators, reported the newspaper, were concerned about the *Titanic*'s use "of the northern course over a route commonly regarded as dangerous from icebergs." A few days later, several faces were reddened when it was found that Captain Smith had scrupulously followed "the southern route" that was theoretically free of ice.

To his chagrin, Senator Smith failed to reach New York Harbor in time to board the *Carpathia* before she docked. Part of his delay was occasioned by his eagerness for headlines, for he spent half an hour explaining his plans to a reporter. "I intend to press for an immediate and deep-reaching search after the causes of the disaster," Smith said. In response to a question, he replied that he did

On the Friday morning following the arrival of the Titanic *survivors, the Senate subcommittee investigating the tragedy convened in the Waldorf-Astoria. The first witness called was J. Bruce Ismay, seen just right of center in the illustration above.*

not intend to interrogate every survivor, since many of them would be interviewed by reporters. He concluded by acknowledging that it was all but certain that "the British Board of Trade will conduct inquiries of their own."

Waving his credentials, the Michigan senator pushed his way aboard the rescue ship while she lay at the pier. Inquiring for Ismay, he was directed to the surgeon's cabin and began firing questions as soon as he had introduced himself. Ismay said he doubted that he or any other British subject could be required to appear before a committee of the U.S. Congress. Smith smiled triumphantly and informed him that before leaving Washington he had consulted the attorney general. His investigative body, he explained, could subpoena citizens of other nations "as long as they are in United States territory."

His secretary having made a reservation for him, Smith went to the Waldorf-Astoria Hotel to inspect facilities that would be made available for his inquiry. Then he prepared a press release announcing that the first witness would be heard on Friday, April 19.

Smith was greatly interested in the stories that some passengers—probably from third class—had been kept out of the lifeboats at gunpoint. Carl Johnson, a steerage passenger, told a reporter that he was asleep at the time the iceberg was struck. He felt "only a slight jar and a creaking," which partially awakened him. Since there was no excitement among fellow passengers he went back to sleep and was later awakened by a pair of ship's officers. They told him to dress and go on deck as "there has been an accident, but there is no danger."

As soon as he got on deck, Johnson "saw the first signs of panic among the passengers. Women were screaming with terror and men were rushing this way and that." The steerage passenger told a reporter, "Suddenly I heard shrieks and cries amidship, and the sharp report of several shots." This was a matter, Smith decided, that needed serious questioning under oath.

CORROBORATION OF Johnson's story, after a fashion, came from a survivor who identified herself as Mrs. Alexander Lurch. She and others, she said, "were forced to sign a paper stating that there had been no disorder of any kind, and that all had been conducted on board the liner with precision." Her story surfaced, reported the *Times,* when friends with whom she lunched insisted that she should make it public.

During a long interview, she told a reporter that her husband went on deck when noises were heard but was assured that nothing had happened and he should return to his stateroom. He did so but could not dismiss from his mind the noises he had heard. After telling his wife she'd better get dressed, both of them went back on deck. There she "saw men passing babies into the lifeboats, which had already been lowered."

Coming to what the reporter regarded as the heart of her account, the survivor said, "I saw one woman clinging to her husband's neck and crying to the sailors to save him. Instead of doing this the sailor drew a revolver and pressing it to the man's head shot him to death. Several sailors then picked up the body, tossed it into the ocean, and threw the woman into a lifeboat."

At his hotel, Smith marked the column that included Mrs. Lurch's story. Later he clipped it and pasted it into a notebook already more than half-filled with other material from newspapers of New York, Boston, Philadelphia, and Washington.

The senator was disconcerted when one of his aides reported that he had not been able to serve Mrs. Lurch with a subpoena. A check of the passenger lists, known to be incomplete and inaccurate, did not reveal that a Mr. and Mrs. Alexander Lurch were aboard the *Titanic*.

Almost as frustrating to Smith was the full hour he spent trying to find the name of the designer of the *Titanic*, whom he found to be Thomas Andrews. Like Ismay, Andrews was aboard the liner to determine what changes, if any, should be made before her second departure from Southampton. Since Andrews was a victim of the disaster, the *Titanic* subcommittee would be unable to learn anything from him.

The Senate inquiry began on April 19 as planned and extended until May 25. Some of Smith's committee members spent only a day in New York and one was reported as having failed to be there for a single session. Possibly for that reason, the inquiry moved to Washington for a time but returned to New York for its last few days. As he planned to do from the start, Smith took the initiative and posed most of the questions. A total of eighty-two witnesses were grilled; of these fifty or fifty-one were listed as British subjects. Half of them were members of the crew who were there under coercion by a federal marshal, having been taken from the *Lapland* just before she cleared the harbor on her voyage to England.

Reporters learned from Smith on the first day that in addition to addressing questions of safety, he hoped to see that the survivors and the relatives of the dead would be adequately compensated for all losses. Fourteen years earlier, lawmakers had reacted to the disaster of the vessel *La Bourgogne* by enacting a measure which made negligence just cause for a lawsuit. To his chagrin, Smith was informed that the Harter Act was not applicable to the case of the *Titanic*.

The first witness called before the committee was Ismay. Smith asked that he describe what had happened "as succinctly as possible." Ismay responded with the distances covered on each day of the voyage and then gave his account of the collision and what followed: "I was in bed myself, asleep, when the accident happened. The ship sank, I am told, at two-twenty. That, sir, is all I think I can tell you."

Smith was appalled at the paucity of Ismay's account and began a lengthy cross examination that totaled fifty-eight pages of

Sen. William Alden Smith called both wireless operators, Bride (above) and Cottam (below), to explain their motives and the details behind the selling of their stories to the New York Times.

testimony. In the end Ismay found himself portrayed as a hostile witness and the scapegoat. His demeanor did little to change those perceptions. Smith was also concerned as to why Ismay had wanted to get the surviving crewmen back to England so quickly and did not accept the explanation that Ismay had the men's best interests at heart in getting them back so they could find a berth on another ship and start earning a living again.

Although the matter was never brought up at the hearings, the press began to question how Ismay came to survive the tragedy and questioned his honor in the face of the others who had no choice but to die when the ship foundered. Ismay tried to distance himself from any role in the running of the *Titanic,* claiming that the captain was responsible for the ship's journey, including the collision with the iceberg.

Lawrence Beesley attended all of the New York sessions, despite his conclusion after the second day that "nothing new is likely to be developed; almost everything told to senators has already appeared in one or several newspapers." The editors agreed with the assessment of the British teacher. Smith was disappointed that the proceedings over which he presided evoked no banner headlines, only stories on the inside pages of newspapers.

Ismay was nettled at the tedious proceedings and long delays, so he requested permission to return to England. Smith indignantly denied his request and in doing so evoked headlines that did him no good. Several major British newspapers devoted considerable space to the "high-handed way in which the American hearings are being conducted." While the editors of the *New York Herald* castigated their English counterparts, the general public showed little or no interest in this transatlantic joust between the members of the press.

To make matters worse, several of Smith's questions were viewed as odd by the British press and were frequently cited to embarrass him, claiming that such questions betrayed his ignorance of things nautical. For instance, regarding the watertight compartments, he asked Lightoller if any of the passengers or crew had sought safety in these. After Lightoller recounted the ship's forward funnel collapsing on a knot of passengers in the water, Smith asked if any were killed. He asked another witness if the ship had sunk by the bow or the head. During the testimony of Fifth Officer Harold Lowe, he asked if the seaman knew what the iceberg was made of.

Smith was not the laughingstock these questions seemed to paint. Instead, he was trying to piece together the story of the tragedy that the common man might understand. In inquiring about the makeup of the iceberg, he was trying to answer the question on many people's minds as to how frozen water could mortally wound the largest ocean liner in the world. Regarding the watertight compartments, he wanted to allay the anxiety of those who envisioned scores of passengers at the bottom of the sea in watertight compartments who would have asphyxiated for the lack of air. To his discredit, he was not always clear in his reasoning, and the fact that he did not delegate any responsibility to other members of the committee but conducted the cross-examination himself only underlined to many his desire to hold on to the limelight.

Col. Archibald Gracie, whose health was seriously impaired by his ordeal at sea, was labeled "a very important witness" by Smith. He testified at length but threw little new light on how the officers and seamen reacted to the news that passengers on the *Titanic* should take to the lifeboats. Second Officer Lightoller, senior in authority to all other surviving members of the crew, was questioned at great length. To Smith and his colleagues, the British professional seaman seemed "rather reluctant to answer questions freely," but he stuck to his previous version of what took place.

Testimony before the Smith committee, however, did uncover the presence of another ship—the *Californian*—nearby the *Titanic* that should have responded to the ship's distress calls. The committee also learned that ships had no standard procedures for conveying wireless messages to the bridge, which in the case of the *Titanic* meant that while several messages regarding ice had been received, they had not been treated uniformly and analyzed to ascertain the ice field into which the ship was headed. The matter of sufficient lifeboats was also discussed and logically called for lifeboats for everyone aboard. Finally, wireless equipment could no longer be treated as a novelty but a necessity that should be manned twenty-four hours a day. In the end, Smith's committee concluded that the *Titanic* had followed standard procedure, thus under existing laws there had been no negligence. The tragedy fell under the category of an act of God.

Scores of lengthy depositions taken outside the meeting place of the subcommittee filled more than eleven hundred pages and were subsequently summarized in its formal fifty-page report. On May 18, 1912, Smith presented his findings to the full Senate and

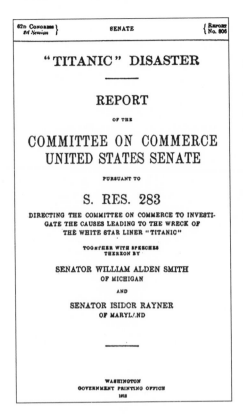

The report of the subcommittee on the Titanic *tragedy was delivered on May 18, 1912, before the full Senate and a packed gallery. It was one of Smith's best speeches and outlined the events following the collision with the iceberg and the suggestions of the subcommittee to avoid future mishaps, including the founding of an ice patrol and sufficient lifeboats for all passengers and crew.*

a packed gallery. He spoke for more than two hours, presenting one of the best speeches of his career. Smith addressed the responsibility of the ship's captain to take steps beyond standard procedure when conditions became hazardous. He also called for routine handling of wireless messages by the bridge crew, twenty-four-hour wireless watches, sufficient lifeboats, and an international ice patrol.

Speaking "on behalf of the American people," the senator from Michigan successfully pled for a special medal for Capt. Arthur H. Rostron of the *Carpathia*. His colleagues voiced no objection when he presented measures calling for an appraisal of the existing regulations having to do with the safety of passengers at sea. In contrast, he condemned Capt. Stanley Lord of the *Californian* for not coming to the aid of the stricken ship.

By the time the Smith hearings ended, nearly all of the identified bodies of the recovered victims had been buried at Halifax or were en route to their homes. Meanwhile, three thousand miles to the east, a second investigation was under way.

Political analysts in Washington and other cities agreed that Theodore Roosevelt's new Progressive or "Bull Moose" political party would affect the outcome of the presidential election in November, and they were right. Those who earlier hoped to "elevate William Alden Smith to a position of first-rank national prominence" were disappointed. When the Republican National Convention met in Chicago's Coliseum less than a month after the end of his investigation, Smith did not play a leading role. Even his most ardent supporters were forced to concede that his skillful use of "a bully pulpit erected upon a disaster" had failed to make him a serious candidate for the White House in 1916.

25

LORD MERSEY

A BLOODY WHITEWASH

DURING NEARLY six years as a member of Britain's House of Commons, Horatio Bottomley made himself heard frequently by speaking out loudly on a variety of matters. To inform the general public about his leadership role, he published and distributed a paper that he called *John Bull*. In its pages he let it be known that he did not trust the American lawmakers who were then inquiring into the loss of the *Titanic*. It would be impossible to get to the truth about the disaster, he urged, without holding hearings in the land where the vessel was built, manned, and from which it had departed on its maiden voyage.

Despite Bottomley's rumblings in person and in print, his fellow members of Parliament showed little inclination to delve into the details about the disaster at sea. Some of them stressed that the tragedy had already brought serious embarrassment to the nation known to rule the seas in 1912. Many of Bottomley's fellow lawmakers resisted doing anything that might give any colonials afar or radicals at home an opportunity to further undermine the crown.

Bottomley not only persisted in throwing out embarrassing questions in his publication, he dug through records and found a report that had been prepared by Thomas Andrews, the designer of the *Titanic*, long before she sailed. According to it, the lifeboat regulations of the Board of Trade were badly out of date—"out of step with the times." They were written when the largest ocean liner in the world was only a fraction of the size of the present ships. Had the *Titanic* been fitted out as originally planned, said Andrews, who went down with the mighty liner, she would have carried forty lifeboats instead of twenty.

219

In the British inquiry into the loss of the Titanic, *the reputations of Lord and Lady Duff Gordon were questioned almost as much as that of J. Bruce Ismay.*

Extremely methodical, Andrews went to some length to note that the *Olympic* and the *Titanic* were equipped with immense davits of a new kind. Naval architect Axel Welin, who had designed these "double acting" devices, was sure that each was strong enough to hold 4 standard wooden lifeboats. Since plans called for sixteen of these davits on each liner, their combined capacity would be 128 lifeboats.

Armed with this information, Bottomley thundered a question that no one in authority was ready to answer: "If the sixteen Welin davits aboard the *Titanic* could have held sixty-four lifeboats, why were only twenty of these craft aboard when she set sail from Southampton?" Members of the Board of Trade, executives of shipbuilders Harland and Wolff, and representatives of the International Mercantile Marine offered no reply to Bottomley's query.

THEY WERE already troubled by the fact that the London *Times* and other newspapers were publishing damaging information.

More and more members of the public were letting it be known that they felt measures must be taken to safeguard travel at sea. Because the tragedy occurred in the North Atlantic, it was the focus of especially scathing commentaries. "Unbridled luxury which makes mammoth vessels pay" was castigated, along with "selection of a track full of ice, fogs, and dangers, instead of a slower, safer track."

Four days after the loss of the *Titanic,* Bottomley served notice that he expected soon to demand from the Board of Trade a statement concerning the exact capacity of the liner's lifeboats. Its president, Sidney Buxton, became concerned that a committee of Parliament might be authorized to launch an investigation. After having consulted Postmaster Herbert L. Samuel, who had oversight of a sort over royal mail steamers, Buxton moved into action to protect his own domain. Before the month ended, the office of the home secretary received a formal petition, begging that John Charles Bigham, Baron Mersey of Toxteth in Lancashire, be named to head a special board of assessors empowered to gather evidence concerning the loss of the *Titanic.*

On the day the petition reached him, the home secretary complied by making Lord Mersey the head of a small body of "assessors" who were "empowered and hereby directed to inquire into the loss at sea of the White Star Line's steamer known as the *Titanic.*" Two of the five men selected to assist Mersey had reached high rank in His Majesty's Navy. Left out of the proceedings, Bottomley could do nothing more than fume in the pages of *John Bull.*

SPACIOUS CAXTON Hall was selected for the hearings, since public interest was high and numerous spectators could be expected to attend them. Under English law, the proceedings were almost equivalent to a civil trial. An immense map of the North Atlantic was brought into the hall, and Harland and Wolff supplied a huge model of the vessel.

With the Smith inquiry in the United States still going on, the British hearings got under way on May 3 with a formidable battery of barristers representing the Board of Trade. The White Star Line brought to the hearings a team of the best legal experts in England. The unions of both dock workers and sailors had their barristers on hand. Steerage passengers, largely ignored in New York and Washington, were represented by two veterans of many courtroom contests. Because their characters had come under serious question almost as soon as they reached New York, King's Counsel Henry Duke was on hand to protect the interests of the Duff Gordons who had allegedly gained command of a lifeboat by means of bribery. Sir Rufus Isaacs, the attorney general, attended nearly all the sessions to give general oversight to them and to frame some of the questions that would be directed to the witnesses. Immediately, he proposed that he and the appointed assessors should take a firsthand look at the liner *Olympic,* presently lying at Southampton, and this was done to his satisfaction.

At Mersey's suggestion, the court analyzed the 1894 regulations concerning lifeboats that were still in effect, every word being studied and its meaning debated. Then members of the crew of the *Titanic* were the first witnesses called. Fourteen of them, whose functions ranged from stoker to steward and from fireman to lookout spent four days on the witness stand.

Mersey next turned his attention to issues in which the ocean liner *Californian* was involved. Numerous newspaper stories, based upon recollections of survivors and crewmen of the vessel itself, had suggested that this ship was very close to the *Titanic* on the night of the disaster but had ignored the distress signals and calls for help from the sinking ship. Capt. Stanley Lord, his officers, and several members of the crew fielded as best they could a battery of questions that amounted to accusations.

Captain Lord claimed that he had never been informed that his officers had seen the *Titanic*'s distress rockets, that he had seen only one rocket, that no one vouched an opinion that there were any distress rockets, and that he had only a vague recollection of the evening because he had fallen asleep in the chart room. For their part, his officers contradicted him on almost every point and even claimed that they had informed him several times of the distress rockets. It also became apparent that these officers did not press their captain to act. Captain Lord ruled his ship like a tyrant and offered only disparaging remarks to his officers when they offered their opinions. These men were effectively cowed by their captain, unable to act on their own initiative. They would rather watch another ship sink than run the risk of their captain's fury.

On the tenth day of the hearings, Lord and Lady Duff Gordon were called before the court. Both of them admitted that their lives were saved because they succeeded in getting into a lifeboat whose only other occupants were ten members of the *Titanic*'s crew.

Several crew members of the Californian *were called to testify in Lord Mersey's hearings on the* Titanic. *To a man they contradicted their captain's testimony that he had never been informed of the distress rockets seen by his officers.*

Since the newspapers had broadcast photographs of a five-pound promissory note hastily scribbled by Duff Gordon, it hardly seemed necessary to ask him whether or not he had drafted it while in the lifeboat. He acknowledged authorship of the damning document but insisted that he and Lady Duff Gordon did nothing out of the ordinary in the life-threatening crisis. In total darkness half an hour after the liner sank, the Scottish baronet testified, the men in the lifeboat began grumbling that their pay had already stopped and that "the company will do nothing for us except send us back to London. Not a man of us still has his kit." Moved by their plight, Duff Gordon said that he told them, "You fellows need not worry about that. I will give you a fiver each to start a new kit."

The situation was not clarified by a photograph taken of the Duff Gordons and the crewmen on the deck of the *Carpathia.* To some it looked as if the crewmen were being treated like a private rowing team.

Charles H. Lightoller, the senior surviving officer of the *Titanic*, remained cool and self-possessed despite being thrown what a London *Times* reporter called "an endless number of questions, many of them being repetitive in nature." He did not deny having observed that the *Titanic* began to list toward her port side not long after the iceberg was hit.

Lightoller was emphatic in saying that the liner broke in two before she sank. With her bow going down and her stern rising higher and higher from the water, he was certain that "the terrific strain of bringing the after-end of that huge hull clear out of the water caused the expansion joint abaft the number one funnel to open up." Biles, one of the assessors, who taught naval architecture at Glasgow, interrupted to explain that all large vessels had expansion joints. These were essential, he said, because without them a large ship working its way through a seaway would have limited mobility.

After a recess of a few days, the court heard from Ernest Gill of the *Californian*. Having earlier been grilled by Sen. William Alden Smith, the able-bodied seaman repeated almost word-for-word the testimony he had given while forcibly detained in New York.

Ismay was then called to the stand. During two days, a court reporter's count indicated that he answered 853 questions, slightly more than half the number to which Lightoller responded earlier. Despite the fact that he had been castigated in the American press for having entered a lifeboat while women and children were still on the *Titanic*, the shipping executive was described in newspaper accounts as having "handled himself extremely well."

After seventeen days of interrogating the witnesses, most of whom were questioned on technical matters, Lord Mersey realized that public interest was dwindling and he decided to try to move swiftly to bring the inquiry to an end. Before he did so, the court was startled to hear testimony concerning the strict segregation of classes of passengers and the result of giving priority to first class. A witness responded to a question by saying, "The striking feature which will no doubt engage the attention of the Court is that sixty-three per cent of the First Class were saved, forty-two per cent of the Second Class, and but twenty-five per cent of the Third Class."

LONDON DAILY SKETCH

	FIRST CLASS PASSSENGERS.			SECOND CLASS PASSENGERS.			THIRD CLASS PASSENGERS.		
	CARRIED.	SAVED.	Per Cent. SAVED.	CARRIED.	SAVED	Per Cent. SAVED.	CARRIED.	SAVED.	Per Cent. SAVED.
Men	173	58	34	160	13	8	454	55	12
Women	144	139	97	93	78	84	179	98	55
Children	5	5	100	24	24	100	76	23	30
Total	322	202	63	277	115	42	709	176	25

	TOTAL PASSENGERS. FIRST, SECOND, and THIRD CLASSES.			CREW.			TOTAL PASSENGERS and CREW.		
	CARRIED.	SAVED.	Per Cent. SAVED.	CARRIED.	SAVED.	Per Cent. SAVED.	CARRIED.	SAVED.	Per Cent. SAVED.
Men	787	126	16	875	189	22	1,662	315	19
Women	416	315	76	23	21	91	439	336	77
Children	105	52	49	—	—	—	105	52	49
Total	1,308	493	38	898	210	23	2,206	703	32

The president of the Board of Trade published an official summary of the number of survivors compared to the number of passengers in each class. Among other things it highlighted the percentages of survivors from each category.

No witness gave evidence that Capt. Edward J. Smith or First Officer William Murdoch had shot themselves, as had been reported in the press. Documents as well as testimony confirmed that though the *Titanic* was overcome by the sea, she had fifteen heavy watertight bulkheads that should have kept her afloat. Designed to be controlled by "powerful electro-magnets," doors could be dropped manually in case of a power failure. In addition, witness after witness affirmed that on a clear night, ice is visible at a distance of about five miles.

With the inquiry about to end, the attorney general asked permission to introduce newly discovered evidence. He produced a document that he said identified six persons in first class who boarded too late to have their names included in the passenger list. When the names of these persons were duly recorded, the court ruled that 711 persons survived the disaster.

After questions and answers had been recorded for thirty-six days at the rate of nearly eight hundred per day, Mersey's gavel put an end to them. The findings of the wreck commission were delivered on June 30. Captain Rostron of the *Carpathia* was heartily commended, but Captain Lord of the *Californian* was castigated for not having rushed to the rescue. More watertight compartments and more lifeboats were recommended, but the investigative body did not have the authority to issue any requirements. Mersey and his colleagues ventured to suggest that lookouts should have their eyes examined regularly. Both Duff Gordon and Ismay were exonerated of the charges of misconduct. "Loss of the said liner," the assessors solemnly ruled in conclusion, "was due to a collision with an iceberg, brought about by the excessive speed at which she was being navigated."

Before the hearings drew to an end, the *London Daily Telegraph* informed its readers that the commission "was not in the ordinary sense a court of justice." If a court of justice should rule some time in the future that White Star and International Mercantile Marine were guilty of "fault or privity," the article continued, limitations stipulated by the Merchant Shipping Act would be negated. Under terms of that act, the liability of owners and operators of the *Titanic* could not exceed fifteen pounds per ton for loss of life and eight pounds per ton for loss of cargo.

A cartoonist had the last word. He produced a sketch in which the findings of the body headed by Mersey were ridiculed as "A Bloody Whitewash." The British public accepted and echoed this verdict for many years.

26

AFTERMATH

RAISE THE TITANIC

I KNOW you are busy, so I will be brief."

"There's no need to be in great haste; you would not be here unless you were on a mission of some importance," J. Pierpont Morgan responded.

"It's very important—the *Titanic*."

"Nothing that I ever controlled gave me greater pleasure—or more pain and anguish."

"I'm not referring to the disaster," Sen. Simon Guggenheim explained. "Some of the families whose loved ones went down with the liner have had a few informal talks, then came to me because I am familiar with the use of heavy equipment. Although I am not greatly interested personally, for the sake of these families I hope you will lead an effort to bring the ship up from the bottom some time in the next year or so. They have consulted the Merritt and Chapman Wrecking Company but are not satisfied with what they have learned there."

Morgan, normally quiet and restrained, seemed as though he would never respond, and Guggenheim took this as a good sign. "Money is no object," he continued. "The families who want to raise the vessel are ready to spend whatever it takes to do the job."

"Do you know the depth of the water where the ship lies?"

"From what the papers say, quoting naval experts, I believe the wreck lies two miles under the surface."

"Closer to two and a half." Leaning slightly forward, the most prominent international banker in the world posed a question of his own. "Do you have any idea what the water pressure is at such a depth?"

"It's bound to be tremendous, but I had not been informed precisely," Guggenheim admitted. "Does that mean you will not guide our undertaking?"

"The pearl of the International Mercantile Marine and the White Star Line is now in a universe of her own. No human can possibly descend to even a fraction of her depth. Nothing that man can ever devise will survive the pressure where she lies." Gesturing with his cigar, Morgan brought the brief session to a close. "Give it up. It cannot be done. Don't try to disturb what is left of her; anyone who attempts to do so will sign his own death warrant before he starts his descent."

MRS. CHARLES M. HAYS, the surviving Wideners, and other members of America's wealthiest families were greatly disappointed at Morgan's verdict. Vincent Astor allegedly considered a plan to blow the wreck of the *Titanic* to the surface by means of powerful explosives. "Perhaps some other tangible things can be done to keep the memory of the disaster fresh in the minds of people everywhere," Clara Hays ventured.

There was no chance that the tragedy would be forgotten quickly as memorial postcards, sheet music, and books began pouring from the country's printing presses. As Mrs. George D. Widener began planning a memorial library for her son, smaller memorials were being erected in many places. One of these, a standing stone in the ancient English town of Godalming, commemorated the memory of Marconi operator John G. "Jack" Phillips.

Special services were held in Saint Patrick's Cathedral in New York as well as in London's Westminster Abbey and Saint Paul's Cathedral. Throughout the British Isles and in numerous American cities, musical groups gave benefit performances to raise money for the families of the victims. Seven noted conductors took their orchestras to London's Royal Albert Hall and combined them for a memorial concert in honor of the musicians who died aboard the *Titanic*. Like the Marconi operators, these men were not members of the ship's crew; they had contracted with the White Star Line to provide music for the round-trip voyage. Incredibly, not a man among them laid his instrument aside and tried to save his life as the liner slowly settled into her watery grave.

As a result of the disaster, in 1913 representatives from a dozen nations met in London for the First International Convention for Safety of Life at Sea. The delegates recommended that their

The captain and crew of the Carpathia *honored Maggie Brown with a loving cup for her leadership and heroism on the sea between the sinking of the* Titanic *and the rescue of her lifeboat.*

respective governments should strengthen their regulations concerning lifeboats and make sure that every liner carried enough to accommodate everyone aboard. They urged the universal adoption of regulations that would require the masters of these vessels to hold lifeboat drills on every ocean voyage. Testimony in the United States and in England had suggested that the liner *Californian* could have reached the *Titanic* before she sank if her Marconi operator had been on duty. An around-the-clock radio watch on all oceangoing vessels was urged and was immediately implemented by many owners of shipping lines.

To minimize future danger from icebergs, an International Ice Patrol was created. This new safety measure was assigned to the Coast Guard in the United States and to the Board of Trade in England. Before the end of the 1913 iceberg season, the American vessels *Birmingham* and *Chester* and the British *Scotia* had each spent two months informing liners about the coordinates of floating mountains of ice. Since the patrol was formally organized in 1914, no lives have been lost in the North Atlantic because of ice.

WORLD WAR I and the Great Depression so dominated life and thought for two decades that little public interest was shown in the *Titanic* story until a stage play based upon the voyage led to a 1930 film entitled *Atlantic*. Laced with heavy doses of fiction, a movie version of Noel Coward's *Cavalcade* failed to win large audiences. In Hitler's Germany a 1938 film entitled *Titanic* carried a heavy-handed National Socialist message. The only German officer aboard the liner was made the central character in a film that had little semblance to reality. The officer pleads with the arrogant, overbearing British captain to slow down when the ship enters the ice field. After the vessel collided with the iceberg, this same officer takes command and ruthlessly decides who will and who will not be allowed into the lifeboats. In 1953 a film featuring Barbara Stanwyck, Clifton Webb, Richard Basehart, and Robert Wagner was an imaginative treatment that was condemned by *Titanic* historians except for its depiction of the dilemma of the third-class passengers who did not know how to reach the lifeboats.

Then in 1955 Walter Lord's *A Night to Remember* became a bestseller. Lord had spent years finding and interviewing people who were involved in the events and did his best to separate fiction from fact. Still one of the finest books about the liner and its fate that has been written, it was adapted for television's Kraft Theater before being made a memorable motion picture in 1958. To date Lord's book has never been out of print.

Clive Cussler's best-selling novel was the basis of another movie, *Raise the Titanic!* Theatergoers who saw it in 1980 were intrigued to learn that its producers had used a fifty-five-foot model developed from the vessel's actual plans. Meanwhile, the real *Titanic* lay undisturbed in an underwater world of its own and seemed likely to remain so for all time to come.

ON SEPTEMBER 1, 1985, underwater explorer Robert Ballard discovered the wreck of the *Titanic* on the ocean floor. Ten months later, on July 13, 1986, he broke through the mystery that had concealed the *Titanic* for nearly seventy-five years. Using the manned submersible *Alvin* and a remote-controlled camera pod called *Jason Jr.*, the scientist from Woods Hole Oceanographic Institute photographed the wreck of the liner.

On April 14, 1919, The Seaman's Institute in New York unveiled a tablet commemoratng the Titanic *tragedy.*

Success did not come to Ballard quickly or easily. He first searched for the *Titanic* in October 1977, using a then-radical vessel named *Seaprobe* that had been developed by Alcoa Aluminum. Having the general appearance of an oil rig, this search and recovery vessel was equipped with sixty thousand pounds of pipe whose sections could be attached to one another. An equipment probe at the tip of the pipe was expected to function at great depths. It might have worked had the metal equipment of the *Seaprobe* been as strong as its builders thought. After the vessel reached a spot believed to be near the wreckage, a reinforced section crumpled under the pressure and about three thousand feet of heavy-duty pipe fell to the ocean floor.

The failure of the *Seaprobe* did not quench interest in the search but served as a challenge, and numerous creative minds responded to news of Ballard's failure. Just seven months later, executives at Walt Disney Productions and at *National Geographic* considered pooling their resources for another search. Preliminary studies of underwater photography were conducted by Alcoa's eighty-ton all-aluminum submersible *Aluminaut,* but a cost analysis of the project led to its being shelved before the year ended.

*The greatest maritime
disaster of the century was
memorialized in music within
weeks of the catastrophe.*

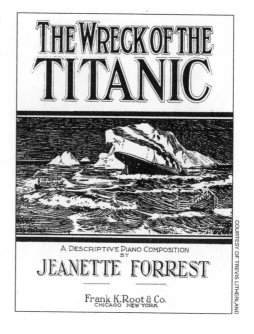

THE WRECK OF THE
TITANIC

A DESCRIPTIVE PIANO COMPOSITION
BY
JEANETTE FORREST

Frank K. Root & Co.
CHICAGO   NEW YORK

COURTESY OF TREVIS LITHERLAND

Nevertheless, interest in the *Titanic* remained high among many oceanographers. At Woods Hole, Massachusetts, the Lamont-Doherty arm of Columbia University in New York, and the Scripps Institute in California, staff members began to get excited about finding the lost liner.

Interested scientists, however, were less numerous than treasure hunters. Although records indicate that many first-class passengers claimed that they took their valuables from the safe of the *Titanic* before it was flooded, tales of gold and diamonds aboard the vessel circulated early. Douglas Wooley of England seemed to believe that the vessel carried gold valued at one hundred million pounds and sought the backing of German financiers, but when they withdrew their support the planned salvage efforts collapsed. Fred Kohler of Coral Gables, Florida, constructed the *Seacopter,* envisioned as a deep-sea submarine, but it was never put into service. Texan Jack Grimm, who had made a fortune in oil, sponsored three futile expeditions.

Unwilling to concede that the sea could defeat him, Ballard searched for and found new backing. With the help of the U.S. Navy and *National Geographic,* the scientist put an unmanned four-thousand-pound miniature submarine to use. Equipped with a

Until 1985 the image of the Titanic *in most people's minds was of the ship preserved in pristine glory at the bottom of the ocean and being very little different from the few days during which she plowed the North Atlantic.*

camera, it unsuccessfully probed the ocean's floor for nearly two months. Just after midnight on September 1, 1985, a member of the expedition glimpsed quantities of debris on the ocean bottom. Before the hour ended, he identified one of the boilers of the *Titanic*.

As yet there was no known method by which men could descend to the ocean floor, but work was going forward in France and Russia as well as in the United States. The discovery of the *Titanic* prompted lawmakers to introduce legislation designed to prevent its looting. By the time the measure became law in late 1986, Ballard had accumulated a substantial number of photographs of the wreck.

What Ballard found surprised the world. Many had assumed that the *Titanic* had gone to the bottom in one piece. The extreme cold, extreme pressure, low salinity, and low oxygen were supposed to have placed the ship in a kind of suspended animation. Ballard's photographs showed that the wreck was in two pieces about half a mile apart. Furthermore, rather than finding a near pristine ship at the bottom of the ocean, he found a dilapidated wreck covered with rusticles and collapsing in on itself.

Within a year, a French expedition succeeded in bringing up hundreds of artifacts from the ocean bed on which the *Titanic* rested. Numerous items of glass and crockery were recovered, along with a bronze cherub that may have been among the treasures Maggie Brown was taking to Denver. By this time so much public interest had been generated that the French government produced a two-hour television documentary about the expedition and its findings.

Until now, Ballard had not revealed the coordinates of the spot at which he had discovered the sunken vessel. Aware that they had been leaked to other scientists or rediscovered, in 1987 he decided to make public what a considerable number of persons probably already knew. Instead of having gone straight down after her last wireless call for help, the liner had drifted about thirteen miles as she slid toward the bottom. Ballard's revelation of the actual location of the wreck may have been triggered in part by the intense interest shown when the French-held artifacts were displayed in Paris, Stockholm, Oslo, and other cities.

Stephen Low, a native of Canada, persuaded Russian authorities to make available two recently completed three-man submersibles named *Mir*. With these craft and their crews, Low secured enough footage to produce a 1991 IMAX motion picture entitled *Titanica*. Another manned submersible, the French-owned *Nautile,* took to the bottom a remote-controlled robot called *Robin*. A 1993 expedition using this special piece of equipment made fifteen successful dives and retrieved one of the ocean liner's Welin davits, part of an engine, three engine-room telegraphs, kitchen utensils, a megaphone, and hundreds of pieces of coal from boiler room number one.

By the time *Robin* entered the remains of the *Titanic* for limited periods of exploration, the luxury liner and her tragic end had inspired four motion pictures. Jacques Cousteau, the *National Geographic,* and other persons and institutions had produced and shown at least seven documentaries. Most of these efforts ended with deficits; one of them reputedly nearly brought financial ruin to Britain's film organization founded by J. Arthur Rank.

Despite this dismal financial record, director James Cameron decided the time was ripe for another *Titanic* film. He had been two and a half miles under the surface of the Atlantic to look at the remains of the liner. Thus he knew that despite testimony by trained observers, young Jack Thayer had been right in 1912 when he insisted that the vessel broke in two before going to the bottom.

Aboard the Carpathia, *young Jack Thayer sketched the various stages in which he recalled the* Titanic *sinking, and L. D. Skidman filled in some of the detail. Seventy-three years later, the discovery of the wreck on the ocean floor validated Thayer's depiction of the vessel's breaking apart.*

Cameron was so convinced that he could produce a never-to-be-forgotten film that he worked without assurance that he would be paid for his effort. Except for a fictionalized love affair between a first-class and a steerage passenger, he insisted upon absolute historical accuracy.

Using a precision-made model and working much of the time in Mexico to lessen expenses, Cameron went far over his ever-increasing budget. By the time *Titanic* was released in December 1997, two studios had combined to pour a reported two hundred million dollars into the motion picture. For its filming, the flooding of the liner's grand staircase was faithfully recreated. Hundreds of doomed men and women were photographed as they struggled in the water, and the ship was shown breaking in two before taking her final plunge.

Within weeks after the release of *Titanic,* all box office records in the United States and around the world were shattered; gross revenue from viewers, some of whom saw it several times, soon passed one billion dollars. Cameron was belatedly paid a reputed fifty million dollars for his work, and the movie received eleven Academy Awards.

Scrupulous attention to even the most minute details about the passengers and crew, their surroundings, their speech, and their attire impelled moviegoers around the world to spend more than three hours in the Edwardian era when the fastest and most luxurious mode of travel across the seas was on mammoth but vulnerable ocean liners.

Bibliography

Anderson, Roy. *White Star.* Prescot, England: T. Stephenson & Sons, 1964.

Archbold, Rick. *Deep-Sea Explorer.* New York: Scholastic, 1994.

Bainbridge, Beryl. *Every Man for Himself.* New York: Carroll & Graf, 1996.

Ballard, Robert D. *The Discovery of the Titanic.* New York: Warner, 1987.

Beesley, Lawrence. *The Loss of the S.S. Titanic.* Boston: Houghton Mifflin, 1912.

Berger, Meyer. *The Story of the New York Times.* New York: Simon & Schuster, 1951.

Blos, Joan W. *The Heroine of the Titanic.* New York: William Morrow, 1994.

Bonsall, Thomas E. *Titanic.* New York: Gallery, 1989.

Bryceson, Dave. *The Titanic Disaster.* New York: W. W. Norton, 1997.

Butler, Daniel Allen. *"Unsinkable": The Full Story of RMS Titanic.* Mechanicsburg, Pa.: Stackpole, 1998.

Coe, Douglas. *Marconi.* New York: Julian Mesner, 1943.

———. *Wireless Radio.* Jefferson, N.C.: McFarland, 1996.

Costello, Mary. *Titanic Town.* New York: Methuen, 1992.

Cowles, Virginia. *The Astors.* New York: Knopf, 1979.

Dunlop, Orrin E. *Marconi.* Reprint; New York: Arno, 1971.

Eaton, John P., and Charles A. Haas. *Titanic.* 2d ed. New York: Norton, 1998.

Frank, Beryl. *Great Disasters.* New York: Galahad, 1981.

Gardner, Martin ed., *The Wreck of the Titanic Foretold?* Buffalo: Prometheus, 1986.

Geddes, Keith. *Guglielmo Marconi.* London: H.M.S.O., 1974.

Gracie, Archibald. *The Truth About the Titanic.* New York: Mitchel Kinnerly, 1913.

Hagedorn, Hermann. *The Roosevelt Family.* New York: Macmillan, 1954.

Harper, Edith K. *Stead—the Man.* London: Ryder, 1914.

Heyer, Paul. *Titanic Legacy.* Westport, Conn.: Praeger, 1995.

Hoffman, William, and Jack Grimm. *Beyond Reach.* New York: Beaufort, 1982.

Kennett, Frances. *The Greatest Disasters of the 20th Century.* London: Cavendish, 1975.

Lightoller, Charles H. *Titanic and Other Ships.* London: Nicholson and Watson, 1935.

London Daily Mirror, April-July, 1912.

London Daily Sketch, April-July, 1912.

Lord, Walter. *A Night to Remember.* New York: Holt, 1955.

———. *The Illustrated Night to Remember.* New York: Holt, Rinehart & Winston, 1976.

———. *The Night Lives On.* New York: Morrow, 1986.

Lynch, Don. *Titanic: An Illustrated History.* Illustrated by Ken Marschall. New York: Hyperion, 1992.

McCullogh, David. *Mornings on Horseback.* New York: Simon and Schuster, 1981.

Marcus, Geoffrey. *The Maiden Voyage.* London: Allen and Unwin, 1969.

Maxtone-Graham, John. *The Only Way to Cross.* New York: Macmillan, 1972.

Miller, Nathan. *Theodore Roosevelt.* New York: Morrow, 1992.

Moss, Michael, and John R. Hume. *Shipbuilders.* Belfast: Blackstaff, 1986.

Nash, Jay Robert. *Darkest Hours.* New York: Pocket Books, 1976.

The National Cyclopedia of American Biography. 69 vols. Reprint; Ann Arbor: University Microfilms, 1967.

National Geographic. December 1986.

The New York Times. April-July 1912.

Ocean Liners of the Past. Cambridge: Stephens, 1983.

Oldham, Wilton J. *The Ismay Line.* Liverpool: Birchall, 1961.

Padfield, Peter. *The Titanic and the Californian.* New York: John Day, 1965.

Pellegrino, Charles. *Her Name, Titanic.* New York: McGraw-Hill, 1988.

Rostron, Arthur H. *Home from the Sea.* New York: Macmillan, 1931.

Sures, Jean-Claude. *The Great Disasters.* New York: Grossett & Dunlap, 1976.

U.S. Congress. Senate. Report of the Senate Committee of Commerce pursuant to S. Res. 283. Directing the Committee to Investigate the Causes of the Sinking of the "Titanic." With speeches by William Alden Smith and Isidor Rayner. 62d Congress, 2d session, May 28, 1912. S. Rept. 806.

Wade, Wynn C. *The Titanic.* New York: Rawson, Wade, 1979.

Whitacre, Christine. *Molly Brown.* Denver: n.p., 1984.

Williams, Barbara. *Titanic Crossing.* New York: Scholastic, 1995.

Wincour, Jack, ed. *The Story of the Titanic as Told by Its Survivors.* New York: Dover, 1960.

World Disasters. Seacacus, N.J.: Chartwell, 1976.

Index

Illustrations are noted by **boldface.**

239

Webb Garrison is a veteran writer who lives in Lake Junaluska, North Carolina. Formerly associate dean of Emory University and president of McKendree College, he has written more than forty-five books, including *A Treasury of Civil War Tales*, *Civil War Curiosities*, *Lincoln's Little War*, and *Creative Minds in Desperate Times*.